Mary Stuart

Joan of Arc

Mary Stuart

A tragedy
First performance at Weimar, 14 June 1800

Joan of Arc

A romantic tragedy
First performance at Leipzig, 11 September 1801

by
Johann Christoph Friedrich von Schiller

Translated by
Robert David MacDonald

Oberon Books
Birmingham · England

This translation was first published in 1987 by Oberon Books Limited
Mill Street, Aston, Birmingham B6 4BS, England. Telephone 021-359 2088.

James Hogan *Publishing Director*
Andrew Purcell CA *Managing Director*
Robert Weaver MIOP *Production Director*

Produced and printed in England by Kynoch Dataset Limited, Birmingham.
Cover painting by Michael Garady.
Text typeset in 'Garamond'.

ISBN 1 870259 07 6

For Jim Hogan

This translation of *Mary Stuart* was first performed at the Citizens' Theatre, Glasgow, on 18 January 1988 with the following cast:

Hannah Kennedy		Ida Schuster
Paulet		Ciaran Hinds
Mary Stuart		Ann Mitchell
Mortimer		Philip Bretherton
Burleigh		Laurance Rudic
Shrewsbury		Stephen MacDonald
Leicester		Jonathan Phillips
Elizabeth		Fidelis Morgan
Davison		Patrick Hannaway
Melville		Simon Elliott
Darnley		David Monteath
	with	Calum MacAninch
		Adam Maxwell

Directed and designed by Philip Prowse
Lighting Director Gerry Jenkinson
Assistant Director Paul Elkins

This translation of *Mary Stuart* was first performed at the Citizens' Theatre, Glasgow, on 18 January 1988 with the following cast:

Hannah Kennedy	Ida Schuster
Paulet	Ciaran Hinds
Mary Stuart	Ann Mitchell
Mortimer	Philip Bretherton
Burleigh	Laurance Rudic
Shrewsbury	Stephen MacDonald
Leicester	Jonathan Phillips
Elizabeth	Fidelis Morgan
Davison	Patrick Hannaway
Melville	Simon Elliott
Darnley	David Monteath
with	Calum MacAninch
	Adam Maxwell

Directed and designed by Philip Prowse
Lighting Director Gerry Jenkinson
Assistant Director Paul Elkins

This translation of *Joan of Arc* was written for the Citizens' Company and first performed by them at the Citizens' Theatre, Glasgow, on 9 October 1987 with the following cast:

Charles VII	Laurance Rudic
Queen Isabeau	Julia Blalock
Agnes Sorel	Ann Lambton
Burgundy	Peter Raffan
Dunois	Mark Lewis
La Hire	Derwent Watson
Du Chatel	Calum MacAninch
Archbishop	Brown Derby
Thibaut/Talbot	Patrick Hannaway
Raimond/Lionel	Ian Reddington
Etienne/Montgomery	Aaron Harris
Claude-Marie/Falstaff	Robin Sneller
Bertrand/Soldier in the Tower	Daniel Kash
Councillor from Orleans	Christopher Gee
Page to Isabeau	Alan McCulloch
Margot	Eleanor Slaven
Louison	Patti Clark
Joan	Charon Bourke
White Knight	Robin Sneller
Black Knight	Daniel Kash

Directed by Robert David MacDonald
Designed by Stuart Laing · Lighting designed by Durham Marenghi
Assistant Director Dafydd Burne-Jones

This translation of *Joan of Arc* was written for the Citizens' Company and first performed by them at the Citizens' Theatre, Glasgow, on 9 October 1987 with the following cast:

Charles VII	Laurance Rudic
Queen Isabeau	Julia Blalock
Agnes Sorel	Ann Lambton
Burgundy	Peter Raffan
Dunois	Mark Lewis
La Hire	Derwent Watson
Du Chatel	Calum MacAninch
Archbishop	Brown Derby
Thibaut/Talbot	Patrick Hannaway
Raimond/Lionel	Ian Reddington
Etienne/Montgomery	Aaron Harris
Claude-Marie/Falstaff	Robin Sneller
Bertrand/Soldier in the Tower	Daniel Kash
Councillor from Orleans	Christopher Gee
Page to Isabeau	Alan McCulloch
Margot	Eleanor Slaven
Louison	Patti Clark
Joan	Charon Bourke
White Knight	Robin Sneller
Black Knight	Daniel Kash

Directed by Robert David MacDonald
Designed by Stuart Laing · Lighting designed by Durham Marenghi
Assistant Director Dafydd Burne-Jones

Mary Stuart

Characters

Elizabeth, *Queen of England*
Mary Stuart, *Queen of Scotland, a prisoner in England*
Robert Dudley, *Earl of Leicester*
George Talbot, *Earl of Shrewsbury*
William Cecil, *Lord Burleigh, Lord High Treasurer*
Earl of Kent
William Davison, *State Secretary*
Sir Amyas Paulet, *Mary's jailer*
Mortimer, *his nephew*
Count Aubespine, *French Ambassador*
Count Bellièvre, *Ambassador Extraordinary from France*
O'Kelly, *Mortimer's friend*
Drugeon Drury, *Mary's second jailer*
Melville, *Mary's former Chief Steward*
Burgoyne, *her doctor*
Hannah Kennedy, *her nurse*
Margaret Curle, *her lady-in-waiting*
County Sheriff
Officer of the Guard
French and English gentlemen
Guards
Court servants of the Queen of England
Male and female servants of the Queen of Scotland

Mary Stuart

Act 1

[A room in Fotheringay Castle. HANNAH KENNEDY, *nurse to the Queen of Scots, is arguing violently with Sir* AMYAS PAULET, *who is trying to prise open a cabinet.* DRUGEON DRURY, *his assistant, is holding a crowbar]*

Kennedy What are you doing, Sir? More of your insolence?
Don't touch that cabinet!

Paulet Where is this jewel from?
It was thrown down from an upper story window;
a bribe intended for the gardener,
no doubt – damnation take all women's tricks!
For all my vigilance, and my strict searching,
there are more precious things, more hidden treasure!

[Busying himself with the cabinet]

Where that was hidden, will be more.

Kennedy Get back,
you insolent man: they are my Lady's secrets.

Paulet They are precisely what I'm looking for.

[Removing some papers with writing on them]

Kennedy Unimportant papers, exercises
in penmanship, to while away the time
in prison.

Paulet The Devil finds work for idle hands to do.

Kennedy They're all written in French.

Paulet So much the worse!
The language of the enemies of England.

Kennedy Rough drafts of letters to the Queen of England.

Paulet I shall deliver them – what's glittering there?

[He has opened a secret compartment and, from a hidden drawer, pulls out some jewellery]

A royal coronet, set with precious stones,
with a design of fleur-de-lys of France!

[Giving it to his companion]

There, take it, Drury. Put it with the rest.

[DRURY *goes out*]

Kennedy The treatment that we suffer here is shameful!

Paulet While she still owns things, she is dangerous,
anything in her hands becomes a weapon.

Kennedy Oh, sir, be kind. Do not remove the last
ornament from our lives. The poor soul finds
pleasure in seeing these relics of past glory,
since you have stripped us now of everything else.

Paulet It's in safe hands, and at the proper time
it will be scrupulously given back.

Kennedy Whoever would think, looking at these bare walls,
a queen lived here? Where is the canopy
over her throne? Must she set her foot,
so tender, so accustomed to soft comfort,
on hard rough planks? And pewter at her table,
the meanest noblewoman would despise.

Paulet It's how she served her husband, up in Stirling,
while she drank out of gold cups, with her lover.

Kennedy Not even the bare necessity of a mirror!

Paulet As long as she can see her vain reflection,
she'll never cease to hope, and scheme and plan.

Kennedy There are no books, to occupy the mind.

Paulet She was left a Bible, to improve her heart.

Kennedy They even took away her lute from her.

Paulet Because she played her sinful songs on it.

Kennedy Is this a life for one so gently-bred,
who was a queen when she was in the cradle,
who grew up in the court of Catherine
de Medici, in an atmosphere of pleasure?
Is it not enough her power is taken
away: must you begrudge her these poor trinkets?
A noble heart may be inured at last
to great misfortune, but it is distressing
to lose the small amenities of life.

Paulet They merely turn the heart to vanity,
when it should learn reflection and repentance.
A wanton, vicious life can be atoned for
by want and by humiliation only.

Kennedy If her tender youth once went astray,
that is a matter for her heart and God:
there is no judge in England who can judge her.

Paulet Her crimes will be judged where they were committed.

Kennedy Crimes? Her chains are bound too tight for that.

Paulet Not so tight but that she couldn't manage
to stretch her arm into the world and fling
the torch of civil war into the country;
against our Queen – whom God preserve! – she armed
bands of assassins: did she not stir up,
from within these very walls, the blackguard Parry,
and Babington, to the accursed act
of regicide? Or did these iron bars
stop her ensnaring Norfolk's noble heart?
The best head in the country fell, a victim
of the headsman's axe, a sacrifice to her.
And did that terrible example scare
the madmen who strove so eagerly to throw
themselves into the abyss for her sake?
The scaffolds are filled over and again
with new death victims, all there for her sake.
And this will never have a stop, until
she, the real criminal, is killed herself.
Cursed be the day when this new Helen of Troy
was granted English hospitality.

Kennedy You call the Queen's reception here hospitable?
Since the first day she set foot on the soil
of England, as an exile, seeking help,
hoping to find asylum with her cousin,
the unhappy woman has, against her rights
as subject, and her dignity as Queen,
been kept in prison here, wasting her youth.
And now that she has known the bitterness
of prison, she is made to stand her trial
like a common criminal, arraigned
disgracefully on a capital charge – a Queen!

Paulet She came to England as a murderess;
expelled by her own people, and turned off
a throne her own atrocious crimes had tarnished.
She came here sworn to trouble England's peace,
to bring back Bloody Mary's times, and make
the country Catholic and betray it to
the French? Why else should she refuse to sign
the Treaty of Edinburgh, and renounce her claim
to England? She could have been free at once
with one stroke of the pen. But she preferred
to stay in prison, suffer martyrdom,
to giving up that title's hollow pomp.
And why did she do this? Because she puts
her faith in intrigues and conspiracies,
hoping by means of schemes and stratagems
to conquer this whole island from her prison.

Kennedy Your sneers are insults added to her injuries.
To say she harboured dreams like that, when she
is living here, walled up alive, no sound
of comfort, not one voice of friendship from
her homeland reaching her: she has not seen,
for so long now, another human face
other than her jailers' sombre looks,
and now she has aquired another keeper
in the person of that uncouth cousin of yours,
and sees new bars put up to keep her in.

Paulet There are no bars to keep her cunning in!
How do I know those bars are not filed through?
Or if the floor here, and these walls, which seem
solid enough, have not been hollowed out,
to let High Treason in while I'm asleep?
This is a wretched task I have been given,
to guard this sly, intriguing trouble-maker.
Fear jolts me out of sleep, I walk about
at night like a tormented spirit, testing
the castle's locks, the warders' loyalty,
and wait in trepidation for the morning
when what I fear will happen. Still, all's well.
Well! There is hope that it will soon be over.
I'd rather guard the legions of the damned
standing sentry at the gate of Hell
than this deceitful woman.

[*Enter* MARY, *veiled, a crucifix in her hand*]

Kennedy Here is the Queen.

Paulet Christ in her hand, pride in her vicious heart.

Kennedy [*Hurrying to her*] My Lady, they are treading us underfoot.
Their tyranny and harshness know no bounds,
and every day brings some new injury,
some new dishonour to Your Majesty.

Mary Control yourself. And tell me what has happened.

Kennedy Look there. Your coffers forced, your documents,
the only prize we saved, and with such pains!
The last remains of all your jewellery
we brought from France are in his hands, and now
you've nothing left that fits a Queen. All's gone.

Mary Hannah, compose yourself. Such trumpery
is not what makes a Queen. And we need not
become as base as those who treat us basely.
England has taught me to bear many things,
one more will be no hardship. Sir, you have
taken by force what I had meant to give you
voluntarily this very day.
Among the papers you will find a letter
intended for your Queen, my sister, England.
Give me your word you will deliver it
to her in person, and not let it fall
into the double-dealing clutches of Lord Burleigh.

Paulet I shall decide what course is best to take.

Mary Sir, you may know what's in the letter. I
have asked Her Majesty a special favour,
the privilege of an audience with her,
whom I have never seen. I have been summoned
before a court of men whom I cannot
in any way regard as equals, and for whom
I entertain a desperate misgiving.
Elizabeth is of my family,
my sex, my rank – to her alone, a sister,
a Queen, a woman, can I tell without
constraint the inmost feelings of my heart.

Paulet It would not be the first time you'd entrusted
your destiny, indeed your honour, to the hands
of men still less deserving your respect.

Mary There is another favour I have asked,
which only inhumanity could refuse me.
Since I have been in prison I have not
enjoyed the comfort of the sacraments.
She who has taken both my crown and liberty,
and menaces my very life, surely does
not mean to close the gates of Heaven to me.

Paulet The deacon of the town will come whenever . . .

Mary [*Interrupting him sharply*]
I want no deacons, I demand a priest
of my own Church: also clerks and lawyers
to draw up my last will and testament.
The sorrows and afflictions of imprisonment
prey on my life, I fear my days are numbered.
And I must now regard myself as dying.

Paulet Fitting reflections in your present state.

Mary And can I tell whether some hasty hand
will not decide to speed up grief's slow work?
I must dispose of what I still possess.

Paulet That is your privilege. The Queen of England
would not enrich herself by robbing you.

Mary I have been separated from my waiting-woman
and from my faithful servants. Where are they?
What has become of them? Their services
I can dispense with; but must be assured
their loyalty will not be made the cause
of want or suffering.

Paulet They are provided for.
[*He makes to go*]

Mary You're leaving, sir? Again? Without a word
to free my heart from its uncertainty?
I am, thanks to the vigilance of your spies,
quite cut off from the world; no news at all
can reach me here, behind these prison walls.
My enemies control my fate: a whole
long month has painfully dragged by, since those
commissioners descended on us in
the castle here, to set up their tribunal
with such indecent haste, and summoned me,
completely unprepared, without the aid

of counsel, to this quite unheard-of court.
Surprised, and stunned, they made me answer their
cunningly framed and severe accusations
from memory, as best I could. They seemed
to come like ghosts and disappear again.
Since that day no one will address a word
to me; I try to guess what you are thinking
behind your eyes, in vain: I want to know
whether my innocence, the ardour of
my friends, or hatred of my enemies
has triumphed – break your silence, let me know
what I have finally to hope or fear.

Paulet [*After a pause*]
Best settle your account with Heaven now.

Mary I hope for Heaven's mercy – and I hope
my earthly judges will be strict but just.

Paulet You shall have justice, have no doubt of that.

Mary Has my case been decided?

Paulet I don't know.

Mary Am I condemned?

Paulet My Lady, I know nothing.

Mary They like to do things quickly here. Will my
assassin burst in on me like my judges?

Paulet Remain in that opinion: he will find you
better prepared to meet him than at present.

Mary I shall not be surprised by anything
a court in Westminster presumes to say,
guided by Hatton's zeal, and Burleigh's hatred.
I also know the Queen of England will
not dare to go too far.

Paulet Rulers of England
need to fear nothing but their consciences,
and Parliament. What justice has decreed
the power of the crown will execute
fearlessly in the sight of all the world.

[*Enter* MORTIMER, PAULET*'s nephew; without paying any attention to the* QUEEN, *he speaks to* PAULET]

Mortimer They are looking for you, Uncle.

[He withdraws in the same way. The QUEEN *notices it with annoyance, and turns to* PAULET, *who is about to follow him]*

Mary One word more.
If you have anything to say to me.
I can bear much from you, a man whose age
I can respect, but that boy's arrogance
I will not tolerate, and hope I may
be spared the spectacle of his lack of manners.

Paulet I prize those things in him which you despise.
Certainly he is not some soft young fool
whom women's lying tears can turn to water.
A travelled man, he's just returned from France,
and brought his true-born English heart back with him.
Your charms, my Lady, will be lost on him.

[Exit]

Kennedy How dare the brute say such things to your face!

Mary *[Lost in thought]*
In the day of our prosperity we lent
too willing an ear to the voice of flattery.
So it is fitting we should hear the voice
of disapproval now.

Kennedy So low in spirits?
You used to be so cheerful, and you used
to comfort me. I had to scold you more
for being frivolous than I ever did
for moping.

Mary Yes, I recognise it now.
It is the bloody ghost of Darnley rising
angrily from his grave, and he will never
leave me in peace until my grief's complete.

Kennedy What sort of talk . . .

Mary You are forgetting, Hannah,
(but I have a good memory for such things)
the anniversary of that wretched deed
has come around once more; this is the day
that I observe with penance and with fasting.

Kennedy Can you not lay this evil ghost for ever?
Long years of penitence and cruel trials

of suffering have atoned for what you did.
The Church, that holds the key of absolution
for every sin, and Heaven, have forgiven you.

Mary Guilt long forgiven bleeds afresh, and rises
out of its barely-covered grave; the ghost
of my dead husband cries out for revenge
and it will not be sent back to the tomb
by altar-boys with bells, or priests with hosts.

Kennedy It was not you who killed him. Others did it.

Mary I knew about it. And I let it happen.
I was the one who lured him to his death.

Kennedy You were so young. That must be some excuse.

Mary So young, to take on such a load of guilt.

Kennedy You were provoked by libels, bloody insults,
and by the arrogance of the man whom you
had raised from nothing by your love, and brought
from the bedroom to the throneroom, and made happy
both with your beauty and the Scottish crown.
Could he forget his splendour and his power
were the creations of your selfless love?
Forget he did, though, worthless creature, and
outraged your tenderness with mean suspicions
and brutal manners, till he had become
repulsive in your eyes. The spell was broken
which had deceived you, and you fled in anger
from his despised embrace, and left him to
contempt – and he – did he make any effort
to win your favour back, or beg forgiveness?
fall in repentance at your feet? or swear
to be better in the future? He defied you.
Your wretched creature wished to be your King.
He had your favourite killed in front of you:
Rizzio, the singer, stabbed to death,
a bloody deed which was revenged in blood.

Mary And which will be revenged in blood on me.
You comfort and condemn me both at once.

Kennedy The fact that you allowed it to be done
shows that you were not mistress of yourself,
but in the grip of blind, consuming passion
which had enslaved you to the villainous Bothwell,

a lecher who, once he'd imposed his will
on you, fuddled your mind with sorcery,
inflamed your . . .

Mary All the sorcery he used
was his own manly strength and my own weakness.

Kennedy That is not true. He must have called upon
the powers of darkness to bewitch you so.
You would not listen to my warnings, would
not see what you were doing. You had lost
all sense of decency in front of people.
Your cheeks which once would blush with modesty
now glowed with frank desire. You had cast off
all thought of secrecy: that man's depravity
had triumphed over your reserve. You waved
the scandal like a flag in peoples faces.
You let that murderer, whom the people's curse
pursued, parade in front of you in triumph
carrying the royal sword of Scotland through
the streets of Edinburgh: Parliament
you had surrounded with armed men, and turned
justice into a farce when you compelled
the judges to acquit that wretch of murder.
You went still further – oh, dear God you . . .

Mary Say it!
I led him to the altar.

Kennedy May eternal
silence cover that deed: it is so dreadful
I shudder at it still, it was the act
of a lost soul – but you are no lost soul:
I know you, it was I who brought you up
from childhood, and I know your heart is soft,
accessible to shame: light-mindedness
is your only real defect; and I repeat,
there are evil spirits which can find their way
so quickly into the unprotected heart:
once there, they swiftly cause us to
do terrible things, and then make their escape
to Hell, and leave the horror, festering
behind them, in the heart they have defiled.
Since that black crime which shadowed your whole life,
you have done nothing reprehensible.
I've witnessed all the signs of your improvement.

Take courage then, and make peace with yourself.
Whatever you may still have to reproach
yourself with, you cannot be called to account for,
here in England: Elizabeth is not
your judge, and neither is her Parliament.
You are kept here by force, and you can stand
in front of that outrageous travesty
of a court with all the courage of your innocence.

Mary Who's there?

[MORTIMER *appears at the door*]

Kennedy The nephew. Go inside.

[*Enter* MORTIMER *timidly*]

Mortimer [*To the* NURSE] Leave us, and keep watch outside the door.
I have some private business with the Queen.

Mary [*With authority*] Hannah, stay here.

Mortimer My lady, have no fear. You do not know me.

[*He hands her a card*]

Mary [*Looks at it and starts back in amazement*]
Ha! What is it?

Mortimer [*To the* NURSE] Go, Mistress Kennedy.
See that my uncle does not interrupt us.

Mary Go. Go. Do as he says. It's from my uncle
the Cardinal of Lorraine. He writes from France.
"The man who brings this is Sir Edward Mortimer;
trust him, you have no truer friend in England."
[*She looks at him in astonishment*]
Can this be possible? And not some trick
to hoodwink me? Have I a friend so near,
when I had thought I had been quite abandoned
by all the world, and I find him in you
my jailer's nephew, and the man I thought
was my arch-enemy . . .

Mortimer [*Throwing himself at her feet*]
Forgive the hateful mask.
It cost me pains enough to put it on:
and yet I must be grateful to it, since
it brought me close enough to you for me
to bring assistance and to rescue you.

Mary Rise, sir – you have taken me by surprise –
I cannot make the change from misery
to hope so quickly. Tell me, sir, what is
this turn of fortune; can I believe in it?

Mortimer [*Rising*] Time's running out. My uncle will be here
bringing a man I loathe along with him.
But hear, before they bring their painful news,
how Heaven has contrived a way to save you.

Mary It is a miracle to deliver me.

Mortimer First let me tell you something of myself.

Mary Speak, sir.

Mortimer Your Majesty, I had just turned twenty,
the product of srict bringing-up, nursed in
the deepest hatred of Catholicism.
An irresistable desire drove me
to go abroad. I left my home behind me,
the puritanical prayer-meetings too,
made my way quickly down through France towards
the Italy I longed so much to see.
It was the year of the great Jubilee;
armies of pilgrims swarmed along the roads.
It was as if all mankind had set out
on pilgrimage to Heaven, and I too
was caught up in the torrent of believers
and swept along towards Rome . . .
Oh, my Queen, the wonder that I felt
when first the splendour of triumphal arches
and columns rose before me, when amazement held me
captive before the Colosseum's majesty,
and when the lofty soul of Art embraced me
in its miraculous, joyous world! Never before
had I experienced the power of art:
the Church in which I was brought up condemns
all sensuous charm, allows no graven images,
revering only the incorporal, abstract word.
What were my feelings when I went inside
those churches, heard the music, saw the ceilings,
crowded with such a prodigality
of figures, showing to my ravished senses
all that was holiest, most glorious!
Then, when I saw those divine happenings:

the Annunciation, the Nativity,
the Blessèd Mother, and the Trinity
come down to earth, the Transfiguration –
and when I saw the Pope in all his glory,
celebrating Mass, blessing all nations!
What are the gold and precious stones with which
the monarchs of this world adorn themselves?
Only the Holy Father is surrounded
with godliness, his house is not of this world.

Mary Oh, spare me! Say no more. Do not go on
unrolling the fresh tapestry of life
in front of me, a prisoner!

Mortimer As I was!
It was as if I had been freed from prison;
my spirit seemed to break its chains, and taste
the joy of life. I found myself sought out
by many Scottish noblemen, and Frenchmen
through whom I met the Cardinal of Guise,
your uncle. What a man! Assured and lucid,
manly and great! As if he had been born
to take command over the souls of men!
The perfect model of a royal priest,
a prince of the Church – I never saw his like!

Mary Then you have seen him, face to face, the man
I loved and venerated so when I was young?
Tell me about him. Does he remember me?
How are his fortunes? Has life been kind to him?
Still the same splendid bastion of the Church?

Mortimer He even condescended to instruct me
in all the tenets of the faith, dispelling
the doubts that I still entertained, and showed me
how reason finally leads men astray,
how our eyes must see the things our hearts
are to believe, and how the Church must have
a visible head, and how the spirit of truth
hovered over the council of the Fathers.
All false notions of my immaturity
vanished before his overmastering logic
and eloquence. I came back to the bosom
of Holy Mother Church, forswore my heresy.

Mary One of those thousands whom he, by the power
of his angelic words has brought to their salvation.

Mortimer When, shortly after this, his duties took him
to France, he sent me on to Rheims, where the Society
of Jesus keeps up the holy work of training
new priests to serve the Church in England. There
I met the Scotsman Morgan, and your true
and loyal friend, the learned Bishop of Ross,
living their joyless exile out in France.
I spent much time with these distinguished men
to strengthen myself in faith. One day, when I
was looking around the Bishop's rooms, a picture
of a woman caught my eye, of such rare beauty
my soul was shaken to its very depths.
The Bishop saw me look at it, and said:
"It gives me no surprise to see you looking
with such emotion at the portrait of
the loveliest of women, and the saddest.
She is enduring martyrdom for our faith,
and it is in your country that she suffers."

Mary That honest man! No, I have not lost all,
if I have such a friend still in misfortune.

Mortimer Then, with heart-rending eloquence, he began
to tell me of your martyrdom, and of
your enemies' bloodthirstiness, and of
your family's history, and your descent
from the great house of Tudor, and convinced me
you alone were the lawful Queen of England.
And not Elizabeth, the puppet-Queen,
born illegitimate, whom her own father, Henry
himself, repudiated as a bastard.
I did not want to take his word alone,
but canvassed the opinions of all
the learned jurists, studied manuals
of heraldry, and found, wherever I asked,
they all confirmed the justice of your claim.
Your only wrong was to assert your right
to England, to the kingdom where you languish
a prisoner where you should be a Queen.

Mary That miserable title is the source
of all the miseries I suffer now.

Mortimer About this time I heard that you had been
removed from Talbot's castle, and had been
placed in my uncle's custody. I traced

the hand of Heaven in the circumstance:
I felt that destiny had picked me out
to be your rescuer and liberator.
My friends gave their assent, the Cardinal
gave me both his blessing and advice
on how to play the devious role I'd chosen.
The plan was quickly made, and I began
my journey back to my own country where
I landed, as you know, ten days ago.
[*He hesitates*]
And that, my Lady, was when I saw you,
no picture now, but breathing, in the flesh.
This castle's not a prison, but a treasurehouse,
a temple of more spendour than the court
of England. Oh, what happiness just to breathe
the same air as you breathe! Elizabeth is right
to keep you hidden. Every man in England
would draw his sword for you, and insurrection
would stalk the land, if once your wrongs were known,
and Englishmen could see their Queen!

Mary It would
be well for her if they saw her with your eyes!

Mortimer If once the gentleness and dignity were seen
with which you bear these sad humiliations.
For do you not come out of every trial
always a Queen? Has prison marred your beauty?
Lacking the bare necessities to make
life bearable, you radiate light and life.
I cannot set my foot across the threshold
without my heart being torn and gripped with pity
and at the same time captivated with
the joy of seeing you. But now the moment
of decision is upon us, every hour
your danger grows more pressing, and I dare
delay no longer – cannot any longer
conceal from you the dreadful . . .

Mary Am I sentenced?
You can speak freely. I can bear it.

Mortimer Yes.
Forty-two judges have pronounced you guilty.
The Lords, the Commons and the City of London
press urgently for execution of

the sentence. Only the Queen still hesitates –
a subtle trick to make them force her to it:
not a humane desire to spare your life.

Mary [*With composure*]
Sir, you do not surprise nor frighten me.
Your news is only what I've long expected.
I know my judges: after the maltreatment
which I have suffered, I can well believe
they cannot set me free – and I know what
they have in mind for me: perpetual
imprisonment, and my revenge, my right
to justice and my claim be buried with me.

Mortimer Oh, no, Your Majesty, no, no. They will
not stop at that. No tyranny dares leave
its work half done. While you are still alive,
there is no dungeon deep enough to hide you.
Only your death can make her throne secure.

Mary And would she dare to send a crowned head
in ignominy to the block?

Mortimer She would and will.
There is no doubt of that.

Mary And in that way
erode her own position, and the majesty
she shares with all her fellow-sovereigns?
Does she not fear the vengeance of the French?

Mortimer She is negotiating lasting peace
with France: by marriage to the Duke of Anjou.

Mary Will not the King of Spain declare war on her?

Mortimer She does not fear a world in arms, so long
as she can stay at peace with her own subjects.

Mary And is this spectacle to impress the English?

Mortimer Do not forget, my Lady, that this country
has recently seen more than one royal lady
quitting the throne to mount the scaffold.
Elizabeth's own mother took that road,
and Catherine Howard followed her, and even
Lady Jane Grey was an anointed Queen.

Mary [*After a pause*]
No, Mortimer, these fears of yours are idle.
Your loyal heart calls up these phantom terrors.
It's not the scaffold that I am afraid of.
Elizabeth has other means, less obvious,
to rid herself of me. It would be easier
to find an assassin for me than a headsman.
That is what makes me tremble, sir. I cannot
set a glass to my lips without a shudder
to think it may come with my sister's love.

Mortimer Murder, whether secret or judicial,
shall never approach the person of Your Majesty.
Fear nothing! Everything has been got ready.
Twelve young English noblemen are in league
with me who swore this morning on the sacrament
to free you from this castle by main force.
Count Aubespine, the French Ambassador,
is party to the plan, and lends his aid:
his palace is the place where we forgather.

Mary You make me tremble, sir, but not for joy.
A grim presentiment goes through my heart.
What are you plotting? Do you know what you do?
Are not the heads of Babington and Tichburn,
bloody, stuck up on pikes, on London Bridge,
warning enough for you? Nor the destruction
of all those other men who lost their lives
in the same reckless plot, and only made
my chains the heavier? You must escape
while there's still time, you poor, misguided boy:
unless the sharp-eyed Burleigh has already
got wind of you, and placed a spy of his
among you. Leave this country with all speed
you can: it is a most unlucky business
defending Mary Stuart.

Mortimer The bloody heads
of Babington and Tichburn, nailed in warning
to London Bridge are not enough to scare me:
nor is the ruin of those countless others
who met their deaths in previous hazardous
attempts to rescue you. They lost their lives
but found instead their immortality.
Dying to save you, that is joy enough.

Mary And useless: force nor cunning will not save me.
The enemy is on the watch: the power
is in his hands. I am not speaking of
your uncle merely, and his troop of guards.
The whole of England guards my prison gate.
Elizabeth's free choice, and that alone
can open them.

Mortimer You must not hope for that.

Mary Only one other man alive could open them.

Mortimer Tell me his name.

Mary The Earl of Leicester.

Mortimer [*Stepping back in astonishment*]
Leicester?
The Earl of Leicester? Your arch-enemy?
Your persecutor, favourite of the Queen?
And he . . ?

Mary If I am to be saved, then it
will be through him alone. Now, go to him.
Speak to him freely, and as a guarantee
that it is I who sends you, give him this.
[*Taking a paper from her bosom.* MORTIMER *draws back, hesitating to accept it*]
It has my picture in it. Take it, then.
I've kept it by me for a long time now,
but your uncle's vigilance has up to now
prevented me from sending it to him.
But now, my guardian angel has sent you . . .

Mortimer Lady, this mystery . . . can you not explain . . .

Mary Lord Leicester will unravel it for you.
Trust him: he will trust you – but who is here?

Kennedy [*Entering in excitement*]
Paulet is coming, with a gentleman
from court.

Mortimer Lord Burleigh. Calm yourself, My Lady,
and hear the news he brings with equanimity.

[*He leaves by a side door, followed by* KENNEDY]

Paulet You wished today to know your fate for certain.
That certainty my Lord of Burleigh brings you.
Hear it with resignation.

Mary And with dignity,
I hope, appropriate to innocence.

Burleigh I am here as emissary of the court.

Mary Having so zealously imbued the court
with your spirit, you are now become its mouthpiece.

Paulet You speak as if you already knew the sentence.

Mary Since it is Burleigh brings it, yes, I do.
But to the point, sir.

Burleigh Madam, you submitted
yourself to the court of forty-two . . .

Mary Your pardon
for interrupting you so soon, My Lord.
Submitted myself, you say? I never did
submit myself to judgment by that court.
I never could have done so, never could
have done a thing so prejudicial to
my rank, the honour of my people, and
my son, and all anointed princes. Does not
the law of England state that the accused
shall be tried by a jury of peers?
Which of your commissioners is my peer?
Kings only are my peers, and no one else.

Burleigh You heard the articles of indictment, and
submitted, in court, to cross-examination.

Mary Yes, I allowed myself to be misled
by Hatton's cunning, purely for my honour,
and, trusting to power of my arguments,
I lent an ear to all those accusations
to demonstrate their invalidity.
This I did from consideration of
their Lordships' persons, not their office,
which I cannot recognise.

Burleigh Whether or not
you recognise the court is a formality,
which cannot stop the due process of law.
You breathe the air of England, and enjoy
the benefit and protection of the law:
you are therefore subject to its jurisdiction.

Mary

I breathe the air of England in an English
prison. Is that what living in England means,
enjoying the benefits of laws I hardly know,
and which I've never promised to abide by?
I am in no way subject of this kingdom,
but the free sovereign of a neighbouring power.

Burleigh

And you imagine that your royal title
gives you a charter to stir up dissension
in other countries with impunity?
But how could any country guarantee
its national security, if the sword
of justice did not reach the treacherous heads
of royal guests as well as those of beggars?

Mary

I do not say I am above the law.
It is my judges I am objecting to.

Burleigh

Your judges, Madam. Why? You think they were
culled from the tag-rag of the London streets?
Chattering riff-raff for whom truth and justice
are marketable, who will say or do
anything for money, hire themselves
out to tyrants and glad to do it too?
These are the most distinguished men in England.
Their independence sets them far above
bribery and subservience to princes,
and means they can afford to tell the truth.
These are the men who rule a noble nation
in liberty and justice, men whose names
are in themselves immediate guarantees
against unworthy doubts and mean suspicions:
the saintly Primate of all England at
their head, the people's shepherd, Canterbury,
Talbot, the wise Lord Privy Seal, and Howard,
admiral-commander of the nation's fleet.
Tell me, what more could the Queen have done
than pick the noblest men in the whole country
to serve as judges in this royal quarrel?
Even were it thinkable that party
interests might sway the individual
is it conceivable that forty men
of this stamp could unite in perjury?

Mary

[*After a pause*]
I am astonished at the eloquence

of someone who has always been my enemy.
How can an unschooled woman like myself
ever compete with such a practised orator?
Indeed, if these lords were as you describe them,
my cause would be quite lost, and I condemned
to silence, were they to declare me guilty.
But these great names you bring out with such praise,
as if they were to crush me with their weight,
I see them playing very different parts
in the continuing history of this country.
I see the aristocracy of England,
the kingdom's highest, mightiest senators,
like eunuchs in the harem, flattering
the whim of their great sultan, my great-uncle,
Henry the Eighth. I see the House of Lords,
no whit less mercenary than the Commons,
making and breaking laws, dissolving and
cementing marriages, disinheriting
England's princesses today and branding them
with bastardy, tomorrow crowning them.
I see these worthy peers, hastily changing
their firm convictions with each change of crown,
four times in four successive governments.

Burleigh You say you hardly know the laws of England;
you seem to be well versed in her misfortunes.

Mary And these men are my judges. My Lord Treasurer,
I would be fair to you. Will you be just
to me? They say you have the good of England
and of the Queen at heart, that you are vigilant,
indefatigable, uncorruptible:
I will believe it, and that you are not swayed
by private greed, but only by the motive
of both your sovereign and your country's good.
And that is why you must be on your guard
against confusing justice with advantage.
I do not doubt there are, beside yourself,
honourable men among my judges.
But they are Protestants, and partisans
of England's welfare, who now sit in judgement
on me, the Queen of Scotland, and a Papist!
Recall the saying that no Englishman
can grant impartial justice to a Scot.
That is the reason for the age-old custom

of never letting Englishmen give evidence
in court against a Scot, or Scots against
an Englishman. This curious law was framed
out of necessity. These old traditions
should be respected for the wisdom in them.
Nature has cast two races into the sea
on the one plank, unequally divided,
and told them to fight for it. The narrow Tweed
is all that separates them, and its waters
have often mixed and washed away their bloods.
Hands on their swords, and menace in their eyes,
they've stood upon the banks, for a thousand years.
No enemy can threaten England, but
the Scots immediately become his ally:
when Scotland's set on fire with civil war,
then it is England that supplies the tinder.
This hatred will not cool until one Parliament,
one crown rules over and unites the two.

Burleigh And is this great good fortune going to be
bestowed on England by a Stuart?

Mary Why
should I deny it? I confess, I hoped
I could unite two noble kingdoms under
the olive branch, in happiness and peace.
I never dreamed I would become the victim
of national hatred. I had hoped to smother
for all time their long jealousy, to dowse
the ruinous fires of their ancient conflict,
and, as my forbear Richmond brought together
the red and white rose after bloody war,
unite the crowns of our two lands in peace.

Burleigh You chose an evil means to such an end;
setting the land on fire, to mount the thone
through flames of civil war.

Mary That is not true!
By Heaven, that is not true. When did I want that?
Where are your proofs?

Burleigh I have not come to argue.
The case is settled past all disputation.
It is declared, by forty votes to two,
that you have violated last year's Act of Parliament,

and are answerable, therefore, to the law.
It was decreed last year
by Parliament: "If insurrection should
arise within the kingdom on behalf
or to the advantage of any one person,
claiming title to the crown of England,
the law shall prosecute the guilty party
in a capital charge . . . " And since it has been proved . . .

Mary My Lord! I have no doubt that any law
expressly framed against me may be used
to bring about my downfall – then God help
the wretched victim, if the very man
that framed the law, is he that passes sentence.
Can you deny that statute was intended
solely for my destruction?

Burleigh It was to warn you.
You were the one who made a snare of it.
You saw the pit that opened at your feet
yet you ignored the warning and leaped in.
You were in full agreement with the traitor
Babington and his accomplices;
You knew their every move, and from your prison
you organised the plot.

Mary When did I do so?
Show me the evidence.

Burleigh The documents
were recently exhibited in court.

Mary Those copies, written in another hand?
I wish to see the proof that I dictated them,
and that I did so in the form in which
they were read in court.

Burleigh Babington confessed
before he died, they were the papers which
he had received.

Mary And why was Babington
not brought before me? Why the indecent haste
to help him out of the world before he could
be brought to see me, face to face, in court?

Burleigh Your secretaries have both maintained, on oath,
those were the letters you dictated to them.

Mary And on the evidence of domestic servants
I am to be condemned? Upon the word
of men who have betrayed their sovereign?

Burleigh Yet you yourself declared the Scotsman, Curle,
to be an upright, conscientious man.

Mary That is indeed what I thought – we never know
what men are worth until the hour of danger.
Perhaps the fear of torture frightened him
into confessing things he did not know.
Bearing false witness may have seemed a way
to save himself, without much harming me.

Burleigh The oath was given of his own accord.

Mary But not in front of me! My Lord, you have
two witnesses, both very much alive.
Confront me with them, and have them repeat
their testimony once more in my presence.
Why am I denied the privilege,
indeed the right, that you grant murderers?
My former jailer told me of the statute,
passed by this present government, which demands
the confrontation of the plaintiff with
the accused. Have I misunderstood it? Paulet,
I've always found you were a man of honour.
Prove yourself one, and tell me, on your conscience,
is that not true? Is there not such a law?

Paulet There is, my Lady. That is the law of England.
I can't deny the truth.

Mary Well, now, my Lord.
If the laws of England are to be
applied so strictly when they are against me,
why are these same laws to be set aside
when they might help me? Will you answer me?
Why was not Babington brought face to face
with me, according to the law? Why not
my secretaries, who are both alive?

Burleigh Madam, you must not agitate yourself.
Your plot with Babington is not the only . . .

Mary It is the only issue which exposes
me to the rigours of the law, the one
from which I have to exculpate myself.
Keep to the point, my Lord. Do not avoid it.

Burleigh It has been proved that you negotiated
with the Ambassador of Spain, Mendoza.

Mary [*Heatedly*] To the point, my Lord.

Burleigh And that you have conspired
to undermine the country's faith, and to
incite the Kings of Europe to declare
war upon England . . .

Mary And what if I had?
I have not done so, but what if I had?
My Lord, I have been kept in prison here,
in rank defiance of the law of nations.
I did not come to England brandishing
a sword, I came here as a suppliant,
seeking asylum, throwing myself upon
the mercy of the Queen, my kinswoman.
But where I hoped for sanctuary, I met
with forcible arrest, and chains. So tell me:
am I in conscience or in duty bound
in any way to England? And I claim
the sacred right of coercion if I try
to free myself, to combat force with force,
and to stir up every state in Europe
to come to my protection. I have the right
to use whatever means of war that are
considered lawful, honourable:
only from murder, the secret, bloody act,
my pride and conscience both inhibit me.
Murder would defile, dishonour me.
I say dishonour – it would not condemn me
in any way, and nor would it subject me
to a court of justice. Between myself and England
one cannot talk of justice, but of force.

Burleigh [*Meaningfully*] Do not appeal to force: its savage justice
is not exactly favourable to prisoners.

Mary I know I am the weaker, she the stronger.
Then let her use her power, let her kill me,
a sacrifice to her security.
Let her admit though, it is power alone
and not legality she uses. Let her not
borrow the sword of justice to destroy
her hated enemy. Let her not dress up

bloody audacity in the robes of law.
The world must not be hoodwinked with such tricks.
She can have me murdered, but not judged.
Let her give up dignifying crime
by giving it virtue's halo, let her dare
to face the world in her true character.

[*Exit*]

Burleigh She is defying us, and will continue
to do so, Paulet, all the way to the scaffold.
That proud spirit will not be broken. Did
she show surprise at the sentence? Did you see
a single tear? or any change of colour?
She's not appealing to our pity. She
well knows Elizabeth's irresolution.
The thing that gives her courage, is our fear.

Paulet My Lord, her stubbornness will disappear
quickly enough once we remove its cause.
Certain irregularities have occurred
in these proceedings, if I may speak frankly.
Babington and his henchmen should have been
confronted with her, and the secretaries.

Burleigh [*Quickly*] That they should not. We could not take the risk.
Her influence on people is too powerful.
If they came face to face with her, they would
have changed their evidence . . .

Paulet As things stand now
the enemies of England will disseminate
malicious rumours, and the trappings of
the trial will seem a travesty of justice.

Burleigh That is exactly what the Queen most fears;
why could this mischief-maker not have died
before she ever set foot in this country?

Paulet Amen to that.

Burleigh Or died of some disease
in prison?

Paulet How much misery would have been
spared the country.

Burleigh But even if an accident
had carried her off – we'd still be called murderers.

Paulet True. But one cannot prevent men from thinking
whatever they wish to think.

Burleigh But nothing could
be proved and there would be a lot less talk . . .

Paulet What harm is talk? The effectiveness of censure
depends less on its loudness than its truth.

Burleigh Justice itself is not immune to censure.
Public opinion loves the underdog.
And men are always envious of the winners.
The sword of justice, which men wield so well,
is hateful in a woman's hand. The world
will not believe a woman can be just
where a woman is the victim: never mind
that we, the judges, answered to our conscience!
She has the royal right to clemency
and she must use it – if she lets the law
run its strict course, it is intolerable.

Paulet And so . . .

Burleigh [*Interrupting hastily*]
And so we spare her? We do not.
It is precisely this which terrifies
the Queen, keeps her awake at night. I read
the terrible inner conflict in her eyes.
Her lips don't dare to frame her wish out loud.
Her eyes, though, ask the silent, pointed question:
"Is there no servant who will rid me of
this fearful choice: to live in terror
upon the thone, or cruelly send a Queen,
my own kin, to the block?"

Paulet It must be done.
There is no other way.

Burleigh The Queen believes
there might be, were her servants more attentive.

Paulet Attentive?

Burleigh Who would know how to interpret
an unspoken command?

Paulet What do you mean?

Burleigh Those who, if given a venomous snake to guard,
would not preserve that enemy as though
she were a sacred precious jewel.

Paulet [*Pointedly*] The Queen's
good name is such a priceless jewel, and her
unsullied reputation, which I think
can hardly be too closely guarded, sir!

Burleigh When they removed her from the custody
of Shrewsbury, and placed her in the care
of you, Sir Amyas, it was thought –

Paulet I hope,
my Lord, that it was thought best to entrust
the hardest task to the cleanest hands. By God!
I never would have taken on this office,
fit for a common turnkey, if I had
not thought it needed the best man in England.
Do not let me suppose I owe it to
anything other than my own good name.

Burleigh It could be given out the Queen is sick,
that she grows worse, and worse, and finally
and quietly, she dies: the world forgets her.
Meanwhile your name is clear.

Paulet But not my conscience.

Burleigh Even if you decline to act yourself,
you would not try to stop another man . . .

Paulet As long as she is underneath my roof
I'll let no murderer across the threshold.
Her life is sacred to me, no less so
than Queen Elizabeth's own head. You are
her judges. Very well, then. Judge, condemn her,
and when the time comes, have the carpenter
come with his axe and saw, and build a scaffold.
The sheriff and the executioner
may have free entry through my castle gates.
Meanwhile she is entrusted to my care.
And rest assured, until my task is done;
she shall do no harm here, nor come to none.

Act 2

[*The palace at Westminster*]

[*Enter the Earl of* KENT *and Sir* WILLIAM DAVISON, *meeting*]

Davison My Lord of Kent? Is that you? Back already
from the festivities? Is the jousting over?

Kent Did you not go to see the tournament?

Davison My duties kept me.

Kent Then you missed the best
spectacle, Sir, that taste could ever have
devised, or knightly prowess executed.
The setting represented the chaste fortress
of Beauty, under the onslaught of Desire.
The Earl Marshal, the Lord Chief Justice, and
the Lord High Steward, along with ten more knights
of the Queen's command, were charged to hold the fort,
and France's cavaliers came to attack it.
But first, a herald came and in a song
challenged the castle to surrender: then
the Chancellor answered from the battlements.
They brought up the artillery, and bouquets
of flowers, and clouds of precious scents were fired
from pretty miniature cannon. All in vain!
The attacking forces were all beaten off,
and Desire had to beat a quick retreat.

Davison Not the most happy omen, would you say,
for the Frenchmen who have come to court the Queen?

Kent Oh, it was just a game – in real life
I think the fortress will surrender, in
the end.

Davison You think so? I just can't believe it.

Kent The articles that were most troublesome
have been resolved, to France's satisfaction.
Monsieur will be content to practise his
religious duties in a private chapel,
and honour and protect the state religion
in public – if you'd only seen the joy

with which the people greeted the good news!
It's been the country's constant fear that she
might die without an heir, thus leaving England
to wear the chains of Rome again, if ever
Mary Stuart should succeed her on the throne.

Davison That fear can be disposed of. As she goes
to the marriage-bed, the Stuart goes to death.

Kent The Queen!

[*Enter* ELIZABETH, *led in by* LEICESTER. *Count* AUBESPINE, BELLIEVRE, *the Earl of* SHREWSBURY, *Lord* BURLEIGH, *with French and English gentlemen*]

Elizabeth [*To* AUBESPINE] Count! I must commiserate with these
good gentlemen, whose zeal has brought them here
across the sea. How they must miss, with us,
the splendour of the Court of Saint Germain!
I cannot think up such prodigious feasts
of the Gods as the Queen Mother can in France.
An orderly, contented people, though,
who flock around my litter, showering blessings,
whenever I show myself in public, such
is the spectacle I can display with pride
to foreign eyes. The brilliance of the ladies
that flower in Catherine's Garden of Delights
would quite eclipse me, and my homelier merits.

Aubespine Westminster Palace shows one lady only
to the astonished foreigner – but all
that so delights us in her charming sex
we find united in her single person.

Bellièvre Will the high Majesty of England grant
permission for us now to take our leave,
to carry to Monsieur, our royal master,
the joyful tidings he has been expecting?
The hot impatience of his heart would not
let him remain in Paris: he awaits
the bringers of good news in Amiens.
His men are posted all the way to Calais
to carry to his intoxicated ear,
as if on wings, Your Majesty's assent.

Elizabeth Count Bellièvre, do not press me any further.
Now, I repeat, is not the proper time
to light the marriage-torch. The sky is dark

that hangs over this country, and a veil
of mourning might become me better than
the finery of marriage. From close at hand
a heavy blow threatens my heart, and house.

Bellièvre Your Majesty, give us your promise only;
leave the fulfilment to a happier time.

Elizabeth Monarchs are only slaves of their positions.
They may not follow as their hearts dictate.
I always wished that I could die unmarried,
and that my greatest fame would be, that on
my gravestone men would read some day: "Here lies
the Virgin Queen". My people will, however,
not have it so: they are already busy
thinking about the time when I shall not
be here – prosperity today is not
enough, I also must be sacrificed
for their future, and give up my virgin freedom,
my highest good, to satisfy my people,
and have a lord and master forced upon me.
That is how they show me that they think
that I am just a woman, though I thought
I had ruled them like a man, and like a King.
I understand that God is not well served
when Nature's law is overridden, and
my predecessors have deserved high praise
for closing down the monasteries, and restoring
thousands of victims of a mistaken creed
to the obligations of a natural life.
But a Queen, whose days are not passed uselessly
in fruitless speculations, who performs
the hardest task of all, untiringly,
and happily, she surely is exempt
from that decree of Nature which demands
one half of the human race should serve the other.

Aubespine Madam, you have exalted every virtue
upon your throne – nothing remains to do
except to serve the sex, whose nonpareil
you are, as paragon and pattern of
those virtues in which that sex is unique.
No man alive, of course, could ever merit
that you should sacrifice yourself to him. But if
nobility, birth, rank, heroism,
and manly beauty ever could have made
a mortal being worthy of that honour –

Elizabeth My Lord Ambassador, there is no doubt
a matrimonial alliance with
the royal son of France does me much honour.
I tell you, frankly, if it has to be –
if I cannot avoid conceding to
popular pressure – and it will prove stronger
than I, I fear – then I do not know
of any prince in Europe to whom I would
with less reluctance yield my greatest jewel,
my freedom. Let that satisfy you now.

Bellièvre It is our brightest hope, but it remains
no more than hope: my master wishes more.

Elizabeth What does he wish?
[*She takes a ring from her finger and looks at it thoughtfully*]
A queen has no advantage
over the meanest woman of her subjects.
A common token shows a common duty,
a common servitude – it is the ring
that makes the marriage, and rings make a chain.
Take this gift to His Highness. It is not
as yet a chain, as yet it does not bind me,
but it could become a circle that would do so.

Bellièvre [*Kneels to receive the ring*]
Great Queen, upon my knees, I here accept
this present in his name, and press the kiss
of homage on the hand of my Princess.

Elizabeth [*Who has been looking thoughtfully at Leicester during this last speech*]
My Lord, allow me –
[*She takes the blue riband of the Garter from him, and puts it on* BELLIEVRE]
Invest His Highness with
this decoration as I now invest you
and receive you into the duties of my Order.
Honi soit qui mal y pense – let all
hatred between our nations disappear,
and henceforth let a bond of confidence
enclasp the crowns of England and of France.

Aubespine Your Majesty, this is a happy day!
May it be so for everyone , and may
there be no soul in suffering in this island.
The light of mercy shines out of your eyes.

Oh! if a glimmer of its radiance
might fall upon that most unhappy princess
whose fate concerns England and France alike –

Elizabeth No further words, Count! Let us not confuse
two questions quite so incompatible.
If France sincerely wishes this alliance,
then she must also share my cares, and not
befriend my enemies.

Aubespine France would be acting
unworthily in your eyes, if she forgot,
in this alliance, that unhappy Queen,
her co-religionist, the widow of
her King – Humanity and Honour both
require –

Elizabeth In that sense I appreciate
your country's intercession at its worth.
France does her duty as a friend, while I
shall be permitted to act as a Queen.
[*She bows to the French nobles, who withdraw respectfully with the other Lords. The* QUEEN *sits*]

Burleigh Illustrious sovereign! You have today
crowned the most ardent wishes of your people.
Now, for the first time, we enjoy the blessings
you have conferred on us, since we no longer
confront in fear a stormy future. Now
one fear alone remains to trouble us,
one victim only every voice demands.
grant this as well, and this day will secure
all England's welfare till the end of time.

Elizabeth What do the people want? Speak, My Lord.

Burleigh The head of Mary Stuart. If you desire
to guarantee your people's priceless gift
of liberty, and the hard-won light of truth,
then she must be no more. And if we
are not to spend our lives in fear of yours,
this enemy must be destroyed. Your Majesty
knows that not all your subjects are agreed:
there are still many in this island who
adhere in secret to the popish faith.
They are all hostile to you, and their hearts
incline to Mary Stuart; further, they
are in alliance with the House of Guise,

who are your most relentless enemies.
This furious party is committed to
a cruel war of attrition against you,
waged with the most infernal, treacherous weapons.
At Rheims, the Cardinal Archbishop's seat,
they have their armoury, and forge the lightning
giving instruction in assassination:
from there they send their emissaries to England,
determined hotheads, variously disguised.
From there they have already sent out three assassins,
and an incessant stream of newly-trained
and secret enemies emerges from that pit.
Meanwhile in Fotheringay Castle sits
the evil genius of this chronic war,
flinging her torch of love to set the land
on fire; and all the young men in it, whom
she flatters and leads on with hope, until
they would all march to certain death for her.
To set her free is their battle-cry: and their aim?
To place her on your throne. The House of Guise
denies your sacred right, considers you
usurped a throne which you had won by chance.
They it was who seduced that wretched woman
into styling herself the Queen of England.
There is no peace with her, nor with her kindred.
Her life must mean your death, her death your life.

Elizabeth My Lord, your duty is a heavy one.
I know your zeal, your probity, your wisdom.
But when this wisdom calls for blood, I hate it
with all my heart. Now find some milder way.
My Lord of Shrewsbury, let us hear your views.

Shrewsbury Your Majesty has paid a fitting tribute
both to Lord Burleigh's zeal and honesty.
Though I could never claim to match his eloquence
I do not lag behind him in my loyalty.
May I live long, Your Majesty, to be
the people's joy, the guardian of peace.
Never has this island known such days
of happiness, since first its own King ruled it.
But let us hope this happiness is not
bought at the price of our good name.
Let Talbot's eyes, at least, be closed for ever
if this should ever happen.

Is this the time to see her as a danger,
when France, her only friend, abandons her?
when you are about to give your hand
in marriage to the King's son? when there's hope
for a new royal dynasty in this country?
Why should we kill her? She is already dead.
The real death is contempt. Let us take care
that pity does not bring her back to life.
Therefore my advice is: keep the sentence
condemning her to death, in force. She will
remain alive, but in the shadow of
the headsman's axe: the moment anyone
should take up arms for her, the axe can fall.

Elizabeth [*Rising*] My Lords, I have now heard your views, and thank
you all for your advice and interest.
With God's assistance, who illuminates
the hearts of Kings, I'll sift your arguments,
and choose what seems to me the better course.
Here is Sir Amyas Paulet. My good sir,
what do you bring us?

Paulet Gracious Majesty,
my nephew, new returned from foreign travel,
wishes to kneel before you, and devote
his youthful services to you. I beg
Your Majesty to receive him graciously:

Elizabeth Heaven forbid!

Shrewsbury That being so, Your Majesty must find
other, more lawful ways to save the kingdom.
The execution of the Queen of Scotland
is a means to which we do not have the right.
Your Majesty cannot sentence a woman
who is not subject to her jurisdiction.

Elizabeth In which case both my Parliament and Council
and all the courts of justice are in error?
They recognised my right unanimously.

Shrewsbury A majority vote is not proof of right.
England is not the world, your Parliament
is not the council of the human race.
England today is not tomorrow's England,
no more than it is yesterday's. Opinions
change with inclinations, like the tides.
And do not say you are the helpless tool
of the people's will, and subject to necessity.
You can at any moment exercise
your own free will. Then do so now. Declare
your detestation for all forms of bloodshed;
your firm desire to save your sister's life.
Show those who would advise you otherwise
the force of your royal anger; you will see
necessity displaced, and right made wrong.
You must judge this yourself, and you alone.
You cannot lean on this unsteady reed.
Trust your own gentleness to guide you. God
did not frame women's hearts to be severe.
The founders of this kingdom, who allowed
women to hold the reins of government,
meant, thereby, to show severity was not
a virtue in the rulers of this country.

Elizabeth Lord Shrewsbury is an ardent advocate
for England's enemy and mine. But I prefer
advisers who pay more heed to my welfare.

Shrewsbury She has not been allowed an advocate,
and nobody has dared incur your anger
by speaking in her favour. Then allow
an old man with one foot in the grave,
whom the world's vain attractions can no longer

seduce, to take in my protection
this woman whom all others have abandoned.
It cannot be said that passion or self-seeking
have raised their voices in your council chamber:
but why was that of mercy also silent?
Everything conspires against her: you
have never seen her face, she is a stranger
for whom you can feel nothing. Do not think
I speak in extenuation of her guilt.
They say she had her husband put to death,
and it is true she wed the murderer.
A heavy crime: but one which took place in
a time of misery, confusion, fear,
and civil war, where she was weak, and saw
herself surrounded by rebellious vassals,
and so she chose the bravest and the strongest
to shelter in his arms, who knows by what
seductions overcome? Women are frail.

Elizabeth They are not weak. Strong souls and stomachs dwell
in women. In my presence, sir, do not
let me hear talk about "the weaker sex."

Shrewsbury Misfortune was a rigid school for you.
Life did not turn a joyful face towards you.
You saw no throne ahead of you, but a grave.
At Woodstock first, and later in the Tower,
the gracious father of our country chose
to teach you your first duties through affliction.
You were not visited by flatterers there.
Shut off from the distractions of the world,
you early learned self-discipline, and how
to use your mind, to look inside yourself,
and estimate life's goods at their true worth.
That wretched woman has no God to save her.
Uprooted, sent at a tender age to France,
the court of levity, and thoughtless pleasure,
where, in the endless round of dissipation,
she never heard the still small voice of truth.
Vice dazzled her, and she was carried headlong
upon the torrent of corruption. And there was
the empty gift of beauty, too. She could
put every other woman quite to shame.
And by her manner, no less than her birth . . .

Elizabeth My Lord of Shrewsbury, compose yourself.
We are supposed to be in formal council.
Her charms must be remarkable indeed,
to draw such ardent tributes from a greybeard.
My Lord of Leicester, you alone say nothing.
Does that which loosens his tongue, tie up yours?

Leicester My silence is one of astonishment.
To think that they should fill your ears with tales
of terror, fairy-stories which alarm
the gullible people in the streets of London,
to think they should be seriously considered
in the calm atmosphere of your State Council,
and by men of judgment! I am amazed
that this expatriate Queen of Scotland, who
could not maintain her own small throne, who was
the sport of her own vassals, and who was
finally expelled by her own countrymen;
that she should suddenly become a threat
and terrify you from a prison cell!
What in God's name makes her so fearful to you?
The fact she claims the throne? Or that the Guise
refuse to recognise your right to it?
Can their refusal take away the right
you have by birth, confirmed by Parliament?
Did Henry the Eighth's last will and testament
tacitly disown her, and will England

Elizabeth Heaven forbid!

Shrewsbury That being so, Your Majesty must find
other, more lawful ways to save the kingdom.
The execution of the Queen of Scotland
is a means to which we do not have the right.
Your Majesty cannot sentence a woman
who is not subject to her jurisdiction.

Elizabeth In which case both my Parliament and Council
and all the courts of justice are in error?
They recognised my right unanimously.

Shrewsbury A majority vote is not proof of right.
England is not the world, your Parliament
is not the council of the human race.
England today is not tomorrow's England,
no more than it is yesterday's. Opinions
change with inclinations, like the tides.
And do not say you are the helpless tool
of the people's will, and subject to necessity.
You can at any moment exercise
your own free will. Then do so now. Declare
your detestation for all forms of bloodshed;
your firm desire to save your sister's life.
Show those who would advise you otherwise
the force of your royal anger; you will see
necessity displaced, and right made wrong.
You must judge this yourself, and you alone.
You cannot lean on this unsteady reed.
Trust your own gentleness to guide you. God
did not frame women's hearts to be severe.
The founders of this kingdom, who allowed
women to hold the reins of government,
meant, thereby, to show severity was not
a virtue in the rulers of this country.

Elizabeth Lord Shrewsbury is an ardent advocate
for England's enemy and mine. But I prefer
advisers who pay more heed to my welfare.

Shrewsbury She has not been allowed an advocate,
and nobody has dared incur your anger
by speaking in her favour. Then allow
an old man with one foot in the grave,
whom the world's vain attractions can no longer

seduce, to take in my protection
this woman whom all others have abandoned.
It cannot be said that passion or self-seeking
have raised their voices in your council chamber:
but why was that of mercy also silent?
Everything conspires against her: you
have never seen her face, she is a stranger
for whom you can feel nothing. Do not think
I speak in extenuation of her guilt.
They say she had her husband put to death,
and it is true she wed the murderer.
A heavy crime: but one which took place in
a time of misery, confusion, fear,
and civil war, where she was weak, and saw
herself surrounded by rebellious vassals,
and so she chose the bravest and the strongest
to shelter in his arms, who knows by what
seductions overcome? Women are frail.

Elizabeth They are not weak. Strong souls and stomachs dwell
in women. In my presence, sir, do not
let me hear talk about "the weaker sex."

Shrewsbury Misfortune was a rigid school for you.
Life did not turn a joyful face towards you.
You saw no throne ahead of you, but a grave.
At Woodstock first, and later in the Tower,
the gracious father of our country chose
to teach you your first duties through affliction.
You were not visited by flatterers there.
Shut off from the distractions of the world,
you early learned self-discipline, and how
to use your mind, to look inside yourself,
and estimate life's goods at their true worth.
That wretched woman has no God to save her.
Uprooted, sent at a tender age to France,
the court of levity, and thoughtless pleasure,
where, in the endless round of dissipation,
she never heard the still small voice of truth.
Vice dazzled her, and she was carried headlong
upon the torrent of corruption. And there was
the empty gift of beauty, too. She could
put every other woman quite to shame.
And by her manner, no less than her birth . . .

Elizabeth What are their latest plans?

Mortimer They were all thunderstruck to hear that France
withdraws support, to form a firm alliance
with England. Now their hopes are fixed on Spain.

Elizabeth So Walsingham informs me.

Mortimer And Pope Sixtus
has launched a bull against you from the Vatican:
it had just arrived in Rheims, as I was leaving.
It will arrive here by the next boat.

Leicester England
no longer fears such weapons.

Burleigh They can be
a terrible danger in a fanatic's hand.

Elizabeth It was reported that you visited
the school at Rheims, that you renounced your faith?

Mortimer I'll not deny, that was what I pretended.
All from my great desire to serve Your Majesty.

Elizabeth [*To* PAULET *who hands her a document*]
What have you there?

Paulet A letter from the Queen
of Scotland to Your Majesty.

Burleigh [*Reaching for it hastily*]
Give me
that letter!

Paulet [*Handing it to the* QUEEN]
My Lord Treasurer, forgive me –
I was instructed to deliver it
into the hands of no one but Her Majesty.
The lady always says I am her enemy.
But I am only hostile to her faults.
Anything that is consistent with my duty
I will most willingly perform for her.

[*The* QUEEN *has taken the letter. While she is reading it* MORTIMER *and* LEICESTER *secretly exchange a few words*]

Burleigh What can be in the letter? Tales of woe
which we should spare Her Majesty's tender heart.

Paulet She did not hide the contents from me. She
asks for an audience with Her Majesty.

Burleigh [*Quickly*] Never!

Leicester Why not? There's nothing untoward.

Burleigh The privilege of royal audience
is not one we should grant a woman who
has plotted to assassinate Her Majesty.
And any man who's loyal to his prince,
could never give such treacherous advice.

Shrewsbury And if Her Majesty were disposed to clemency,
would you prevent her then?

Burleigh She has been sentenced!
Her head is on the block. It is not fit
Her Majesty should see a condemned criminal.
Once she has seen the Queen, we can no longer
put the sentence into execution,
because the royal presence means reprieve.

Elizabeth [*Having read the letter, dries her tears*]
What is mankind! Turning on fortune's wheel,
how low this Queen has fallen, who began
with such proud hopes: called to the oldest throne
of Christendom, she dreamt that she would wear
three crowns. And now, how different is her tone,
from when she stole the English coat of arms
and let herself be called Queen of all Britain
by flatterers. Forgive me, Lords; it cuts
me to the heart, and melancholy grips me
to see that earthly good's so insecure,
to think the appalling fate of all mankind
should have passed by me, and yet passed me by.

Shrewsbury My Queen, God lays his finger on your heart.
Obey these heavenly promptings. She has done
a bitter penance for her terrible crime.
And it is time her ordeal had an end.
Reach out your hand to her in her distress:
and like the luminous vision of an angel
descend into that grave which is her prison.

Burleigh Be firm, Your Majesty, and do not let
yourself be led astray by human feelings,
however praiseworthy. You rob yourself
of liberty to do what must be done.

You cannot pardon her, you cannot save her.
Do not expose yourself to the suggestion
that you had gone to gloat over your victim.

Leicester My Lords, let us remain within due bounds.
The Queen is wise, she does not need our council
to help her to decide the wisest course.
A meeting of the Queens would not concern
the courts: it is the law of England, not
the monarch's will, condemns the Queen of Scots.
It well becomes Elizabeth's great soul
that she should follow where her heart directs her,
while unswerving law follows its strict course.

Elizabeth Leave us, my Lords. We shall find out a way
to reconcile the impositions of
necessity, with those of clemency.
Now – leave us, Lords. Young Mortimer, a word.

Elizabeth [*After submitting him to searching scrutiny for a few moments*]
You show a spirit and a self-possession
beyond your years. Whoever practices
dissimulation's tricky arts so young
will be a man before his time, and dock
the period of his apprenticeship.
Destiny calls you to a great career.
I prophesy it, and can make the oracle
come true. Is that not fortunate for you?

Mortimer All that I am and all that I can do
I dedicate to your illustrious service.

Elizabeth You've made acquaintance with our enemies.
Their hatred for me is implacable,
their plots against me inexhaustible.
Heaven has shielded me till now, but still
uneasy lies the crown while she still lives,
pretext for their romantic ardour, and
nourisher of their hopes.

Mortimer She lives no more
as soon as you command.

Elizabeth Ah, sir. I thought
I had got to the end, but find I am
no further than I was at the beginning.

I wanted to let justice take its course,
and keep my own hands free from shedding blood.
The sentence is pronounced. What have I gained?
It must be executed, Mortimer;
and I must authorise the execution.
I shall be always hated for the deed.
I must accept responsibility
and see no way to save appearances.
That is the worst of all.

Mortimer Why should you care
about the look of things, if the cause is just?

Elizabeth You do not know the world, young sir. The look
of things is how men judge us, not by what we are.
I could convince nobody of the truth,
and so I must take care that any part
I may have in her death remains obscure.
In such ambiguous actions there is no
protection, except in obscurity.
The worst act is the one you have confessed.
What you do not admit, you have not done.

Mortimer [*Sounding her*]
Then the best way would be . . .

Elizabeth [*Quickly*] It would indeed.
Oh, my good angel speaks through you. Go on.
Finish what you were saying, sir. You are
sincere, you go straight to the point, you are
quite different from your uncle . . .

Mortimer [*Taken aback*]
Have you disclosed
this wish to him?

Elizabeth Yes, much to my regret.

Mortimer Forgive the old man, whom the years have made
suspicious of such enterprises, which
need all the recklessness of youth . . .

Elizabeth [*Quickly*] May I . . .

Mortimer I'll lend my hand: you must safeguard your name
as best you can . . .

Elizabeth If you will come one morning
and wake me with the message: "Mary Stuart,
your enemy, died last night."

Mortimer Depend on me.

Elizabeth And when will I be able once again
to sleep in peace?

Mortimer The next new moon will see
an end to all your fears.

Elizabeth Then fare you well, sir.
Do not take it amiss that I must dress
my gratitude in the colours of the night.
Silence is the god of happy men.
The closest bonds, the tenderest, are those
which owe their being to a secret shared.

[*Exit*]

Mortimer Go, hypocritical, dissembling Queen!
As you deceive the world, so do I you.
Betraying you would be a noble action.
Do I look like a murderer? Did you read
an appetite for killing in my face?
But count on me to act, while you withdraw
behind a public mask of clemency,
while secretly relying on my aid
as hired assassin. So shall I gain time
to make my rescue good. Would you advance me?
You point to some far distant, rich reward.
But even if your favour were the prize,
poor creature, who are you? What could you give me?
I am not tempted by such empty fame.
Only in her, and with her, can I live:
and you have only lifeless rewards to give.
The single highest good that life can grant:
when hearts, enchanted by what they enchant,
forget themselves to find the good they want.
This is a thing you have no knowledge of:
you never gave yourself to any man in love.
I must attend Lord Leicester, to deliver
her letter to him. Hateful errand!
I do not trust that lackey of the court.
For her deliverance mine shall be the sword,
the danger and the glory, my reward.

[*As he leaves, he runs into* PAULET]

Paulet What did the Queen say to you?

Mortimer Nothing, sir.
Nothing – of any consequence.

Paulet Listen to me.
You have set foot on slippery ground. To be
the favourite of the monarch is attractive,
and young men are ambitious. Do not let
the search for honours lead you to dishonour.

Mortimer Did not you yourself bring me to Court?

Paulet I wish I had not. It was not at Court
where our family earned its lasting honour.
Nephew, stand firm, and do not buy too dear,
and do not act against your conscience.

Mortimer Why!
What is the matter? Why are you so worried?

Paulet Whatever promises the Queen makes now
to raise you up – do not trust what she says.
Once you have been of service, she'll discard you,
and in her eagerness to clear herself,
avenge the murder she herself commanded.

Mortimer What murder do you mean?

Paulet Stop this pretence.
I know exactly what the Queen proposed.
She hoped that your ambitious youth might be
more malleable than my unbending age.
Did you agree to it? Well, did you?

Mortimer Uncle!

Paulet If you agreed, you have my curse, you are
no longer any kin of mine.

Leicester [*Entering*] Good sir,
a word with your young nephew, if you please.
Her Majesty thinks highly of him, and
wishes to give him full, sole custody
of the person of the Lady Stuart. She
relies on his integrity.

Paulet Relies!

Mortimer I beg your pardon, sir?

Paulet The Queen relies
on him, and I, my Lord, rely upon
myself and on the evidence of my eyes.

[*Exit*]

Leicester [*In surprise*] What ails the fellow?

Mortimer I do not know – the unexpected trust
the Queen has placed in me, perhaps –

Leicester [*Looks at him searchingly*]
Are you
deserving of such trust, sir?

Mortimer [*In the same way*]
My Lord Leicester
that is a question I could ask of you.

Leicester You had something to tell me privately.

Mortimer Only if I'm assured it's safe to do so.

Leicester Who gave such assurances for you?
You must not take offence at my suspicion.
I have seen you show two faces here
at court – now one of them, of course,
is false: the only question is, which one?

Mortimer That could be just as true of you, Lord Leicester.

Leicester So who is to be first to trust the other?

Mortimer The one who runs less risk.

Leicester And that is you.

Mortimer By no means, sir. Your evidence, that of
a powerful peer, a man of consequence,
could ruin me: my evidence could do
nothing against your rank and influence.

Leicester You are mistaken, sir. My power here
is great enough, save in one tender point,
in which, I now have to confide in you,
I am the weakest person in the court,
whom even the meanest testimony could ruin.

Mortimer If the all powerful Lord Leicester can
so condescend to me, that he can make
such a confession to me, then I must
think somewhat better of myself, and set
him an example in the exchange of trust.

Leicester Then lead the way, I'll follow you.

Mortimer [*Quickly bringing out the letter*]
This is
a letter for you from the Queen of Scotland.

Leicester [*Starts, and grabs hastily for the letter*]
Lower your voice, sir. What is this? Her portrait.
[*Kissing it, and looking at it in silent delight*]

Mortimer [*Who has watched him as he read the letter*]
My Lord, now I believe you.

Leicester [*After skimming through it*]
You know the contents of this letter, sir?

Mortimer No, I do not.

Leicester Oh, come, she doubtless has
confided –

Mortimer No, she has confided nothing.
She said that you would solve this riddle for me.
And I find it a riddle that the Earl
of Leicester, favourite of Elizabeth,
Mary's admitted enemy, one of her judges,
should be the man to whom the Queen of Scots
looks in her distress to save her. Yet
it must be true; your face too clearly shows
your feelings for her.

Leicester First I want to know
how comes it you are so concerned for her,
and how you won her confidence.

Mortimer My Lord,
that's quickly told; I have renounced my faith
and thrown my lot in with the Guise. The Cardinal-
Archbishop of Rheims gave me a letter which
was my credential to the Queen of Scotland.

Leicester I know of your conversion; it was that
that first encouraged me to trust you.
Give me your hand; forgive me my suspicions.
I cannot to too cautious: Walsingham
and Burleigh hate me, and, I know, set snares
and ambushes for me. You might have been
their creature and their tool to lure me to
their net –

Mortimer What little steps so great
a lord is forced to take at Court. My Lord,
I pity you.

Leicester And I am glad to throw
myself in trust upon a friendly bosom,
where I can finally throw off constraint.
You are surprised, sir, at my sudden change
of heart towards the Queen. But it was never
hatred on my side – force of circumstances
made us enemies. You must be aware
some time ago, I was to have married her:
that was before she gave her hand to Darnley,
while she was still the favoured child of fortune.
I coldly spurned such happiness at the time:
now she's in prison, on the verge of death,
I risk my life to see her.

Mortimer That is generous.

Leicester Meanwhile, the shape of things has changed. It was
ambition which made me insensible
to youth and beauty at the time. I thought
her hand too insignificant a prize;
my Eldorado was the Queen of England.

Mortimer It is well known that she preferred you to
all other men –

Leicester Yes, that is how it seemed.
But now, some ten years later, ten lost years
of indefatigable courtship of
a hated servitude – Oh, sir, my heart
must rid itself of its long discontent –
I am called happy. If they only knew
what chains they are, for which they envy me!
Now that I've done ten years obeisance
before the altar of her vanity,
submitted with the meekness of a slave
to every change of whim, and been the toy
of all her trivial selfish quirks, one minute
the object of her loving care, the next
primly rejected, equally tormented
by her favour and disfavour, guarded like
a prisoner by the Argus eye of jealousy,
cross-questioned like a child, and scolded like
a lackey – there are no words for such a hell.

Mortimer You have my sympathy, my Lord.

Leicester And now
to have the prize elude me at the last!
Another comes to rob me of the fruit
of my dear courtship: to a young, active husband,
I lose the rights which I have long enjoyed.
I must climb off the stage, where, for so long,
I shone so brightly in a leading role.
And this newcomer threatens to deprive me
not only of her hand, but of her favour.
She is a woman, and he is attractive.

Mortimer He is Catherine's son. He has been taught the art
of flattery by masters.

Leicester All my hopes
are foundering, and I look among the wreckage
of my fortunes for some plank that I can cling to.
I turn my eyes towards my first bright hope.
Her image stands before me once again,
in all its charm; her beauty and her youth
regain their former rights: and cold ambition
no longer . . . Now the heart compares, and I
appreciate the treasure I have lost.
With horror I can see her fallen to
the depths of degradation, by my fault.
Then the hope woke in me, whether I might
not still deliver her, and make her mine.
By means of a royal servant I contrived
to inform her of my altered state of mind.
This letter which you brought me has assured me
that she forgives me, and she gives herself
to me, if I can be her rescuer.

Mortimer But you have done nothing yet to rescue her.
You let her be condemned, you let it happen,
you even voted for her death yourself.
It took a miracle – the light of truth
had to touch me, the nephew of her gaoler.
And Heaven, in the Vatican, in Rome,
picked out the unexpected saviour,
or she would never have found the way to you.

Leicester Ah, that has cost me agonies enough!
That was the last time she was removed
from Talbot's castle, up to Fotheringay,

and the harsh supervision of your uncle.
All roads to her were blocked; I had to go
on persecuting her before the world.
But do not imagine that I would have let her
go to a miserable death. No, I had hoped,
and still hope, to be able to prevent
the worst, until we find some way to save her.

Mortimer The way is found. Your confidence in me
deserves no less from me. I shall free her.
That is why I am herc. All is prepeared.
Your powerful support assures success.

Leicester What was that? You alarm me. Do you mean . . .

Mortimer I mean to break into her prison, by force.
I have those who will help me. All is ready.

Leicester Accomplices? Who know the plan? Great God,
what harebrained scheme have you involved me in?
And do these gentlemen know of me too?

Mortimer No fear of that. The plan was formed without you.
And it would have been carried out without you,
if she had not insisted she must owe
her liberty to you.

Leicester Does that mean you
can absolutely guarantee my name
was never mentioned by you to your colleagues?

Mortimer Depend on it. Why are you suspicious
at news which brings you such much-needed help?
You wish to rescue Mary Stuart and make
her yours: and yet when help drops from the sky,
suddenly, unexpectedly, you show
a good deal more embarrassment than joy.

Leicester We cannot do it by force. The enterprise
is far too dangerous.

Mortimer Less so than delay.

Leicester I tell you, sir, we cannot take the risk.

Mortimer [*Bitter*] You cannot take it, who wish to possess her.
We merely wish to save her, and are therefore
not quite so circumspect –

Leicester Young man, you are
too rash for such a dangerous, thorny business.

Mortimer You are – too cautious in affairs of honour.

Leicester I see the nets and snares surrounding us.

Mortimer I feel the courage to break through them all.

Leicester Such courage is insanity, mere frenzy.

Mortimer Your sanity could not be called heroic.

Leicester You clearly want to end like Babington.

Mortimer You, clearly, <u>not</u> to be as brave as Norfolk.

Leicester Norfolk did not survive to bring his bride home

Mortimer No, but he proved that he was worthy of her.

Leicester If we are lost, we pull her down with us.

Mortimer If we risk nothing, she cannot be saved.

Leicester You do not think, you do not listen, your
impetuosity will ruin things
just as our road seemed clear.

Mortimer Would that have been
a road you cleared? What have you done to save her?
If I were criminal enough to kill her,
as the Queen commanded me to do,
and as she is expecting me to do ,
tell me what you would do to save her life?

Leicester Who gave that order? Did you say the Queen?

Mortimer She is deceived in me, as Mary is
in you.

Leicester Did you agree to do it? Did you?

Mortimer Yes, to prevent her finding other hands,
I offered her my own.

Leicester It was well done.
This will gain time for us. She counts on you
to do her bloody work for her. Meanwhile
sentence of death will not be carried out,
and we gain time.

Mortimer [*Impatient*] No, time is what we lose.

Leicester She counts on you, and will not hesitate
to make a public show of clemency.
Perhaps, if I can find means to persuade her

to meet her adversary face to face,
that step would tie her hands. Burleigh was right.
Sentence of death could not be carried out
once she has seen her. I will try my utmost.

Mortimer And what will that achieve? When she discovers
I have deceived her, and that Mary Stuart
is still alive, things will be as before.
Mary will not be freed. The best that she
can hope for is lifelong imprisonment.
You must employ your courage in the end,
why not at the beginning? All the power
is in your hands, you could convene an army,
simply by arming the nobility: although
they may have lost their chiefs, they still are rich
in heroes, men who only long to find
a leader whose example they can follow.
Then throw off this pretence, deal openly.
Defend your mistress nobly as her champion.
As for Elizabeth, you are her master
whenever you choose to be. Invite the Queen
to one of your castles, where she has, God knows,
pursued you before now. Then show her who
is master. Keep her there, a prisoner,
until she has released the Queen of Scots.

Leicester I am astounded and appalled – where will
your lunatic incaution take you next?
Do you know where you are? Do you know how
things are at court? Do you know how our spirits
are curbed and shackled in this woman's kingdom?
Just look for that heroic spirit which
was seen in England in days long gone by.
You will not find it – it is locked away;
a woman holds the key. The springs of courage
have all run down. Reflect before you act.
Some one is coming. Go!

Mortimer The Queen still hopes.
Must I return to her with empty hands?

Leicester Take her the firm assurance of my love.

Mortimer Take it yourself. I offered you my aid,
to be her rescuer, not your go-between.

[*Exit*]

Elizabeth [*Entering*] Who was that left you? I heard someone speaking.

Leicester [*Hearing her voice, he wheels round, startled*]
Mortimer.

Elizabeth What is the matter, Leicester?
You look surprised . . .

Leicester [*Pulling himself together*]
At how you look. I have
never seen you so beautiful before.

Elizabeth Why do you sigh?

Leicester Have I not reason to?
To see you look like that is to make me feel
the loss I suffer.

Elizabeth And what loss is that?

Leicester Your heart, your dear, dear self is what I lose.
You will soon be lying in the arms
of a young, ardent husband, who will take
possession of you unconditionally.
He is of royal blood, and I am not,
yet I defy the world to find another
who could adore you more than I. Anjou
has never seen you: he can only love
your fame, the glittering outside. I love you!
Had you been born the meanest shepherdess,
and I the greatest prince on earth, I'd stoop
to lay my diadem before your feet.

Elizabeth Pity me, Leicester, do not scold me. I
may not consult my heart. It would have chosen
differently for me. Oh, how I envy
those women who are free to raise the men
they love to their own level. I am not
so happy, since I cannot place the crown
upon the head of the man I love. But she
could follow her inclination where she pleased,
do what she pleased, and marry whom she pleased.
She drained the last drop from the cup of pleasure.

Leicester And now she drains the bitter cup of sorrow.

Elizabeth She never cared a straw what people thought.
She found life easy, never cared to shoulder
my burden of responsibility.

Yet I too could have claimed the right to enjoy
the pleasures of this world, the joy of life:
but I chose the stern duties of a Queen.
Yet she was irresistible to men
because she was content to be a woman;
young and old alike paid court to her.
That is what men are like, a sex of rakes
drawn into the pursuit of pleasure, not
able to value what they should admire.
You saw how even old Talbot grew much younger.
when he began dilating on her charms.

Leicester Forgive him: he was once her gaoler. She
has turned his head with flattery and cunning.

Elizabeth But is it really true? Is she so beautiful?
I have to listen to so much about
that face, I long to know what to believe.
Portraits can flatter and descriptions lie:
I will believe only what I see myself.
Why do you look at me like that?

Leicester I was
comparing you with Mary in my mind.
I'll not deny, I should be greatly pleased
if it were possible to see the two
of you brought together – quite in secret.
Then for the first time you could taste your triumph
and she could taste humiliation,
at seeing with the sharpened eyes of envy
how far you are superior to her
in regal bearing, as in other virtues.

Elizabeth She's younger.

Leicester Younger! One would hardly think so.
Of course her sorrows may have prematurely
aged her. And what will make the insult worse
would be to see you as a bride! She has
all her fair hopes of life behind her now,
and she would see you walking towards happiness!
And with the King of France's son, while she
has always been so proud, and made such play
with her high French connections: even now
she boasts she has the strong support of France.

Elizabeth [*Casually*] They nag and pester me to have this meeting.

Leicester [*Urgently*] She asks it as a favour; grant it as
a punishment. She'd rather let herself
be led by you to the block than see herself
extinguished by your beauty. That would be
worse than death for her who planned your death.
Once she has seen your beauty, closely guarded
by modesty, made glorious by a stainless
reputation, such as she threw away
in favour of frivolity and lust,
transfigured by the splendour of the crown,
made fairer by the radiance of a bride,
the hour of ruin will have struck for her.
And as I see you now, you never were
better prepared for such a duel of beauty.
What if you were to go at once, just
as you are, there is no better time . . .

Elizabeth Now – no – no – Leicester – no – not now – I must
have time to think, to see Lord Burleigh . . .

Leicester Burleigh!
His mind runs on advantages of state
but you have your advantages as a woman:
and that advantage is for you to judge,
not for a statesman – though raison d'état
demands that you should meet her, it would be
a generous nod in the direction of
public opinion, and you may dispose
of your hated enemy at a later date
whatever way you will.

Elizabeth It would not be
correct for me to see her if she is
in want or degradation. I am told
she is but wretchedly attended. I
could not see that without construing it
as a reproach to me.

Leicester You do not need
to cross her threshold. Here is my advice.
Things could not have fallen out more happily.
Today the great hunt will pass through the grounds
of Fotheringay, where the Lady Stuart
may take the air. You pass, by purest chance:
it need not, must not seem to be contrived,
and, if you should think better of it, you
need not address a word to her.

Elizabeth If this
is folly that I am committing, Leicester,
then it is yours, not mine. I can deny
no wish of yours today, because today,
of all my subjects, it is you that I
have hurt most bitterly.
[*Looks at him tenderly*]
An odd whim. Still,
our inclinations often make us grant
favours which, but for them, we might not want.

[LEICESTER *throws himself at her feet. The curtain falls*]

Act 3

[Fotheringay. A Park. Trees in the foreground, an open landscape behind]

[Enter MARY *from behind the trees, running.* KENNEDY *follows slowly]*

Kennedy My Lady, wait, you are too fast for me.

Mary Let me enjoy my new-found freedom. Let
me be a child again, and be one with me;
let us run through the grass and quite forget
that we were ever in captivity.

Kennedy Oh, my dear Lady, your imprisonment
has only been a little bit enlarged.
You cannot see the walls that close us in
only because the trees are hiding them.

Mary Then they have earned my gratitude, those trees
that hide the grim walls of our hateful prison:
I want to dream of freedom, joy and ease,
why do you wake me from so sweet a vision?
Is this not Heaven's vault that shelters me,
extending further than the eye can see,
upward to measureless infinities?
There, where the mountain tops begin to rise,
that is my country's boundary.
The clouds scud by us, seeking southern skies,
the warmer shores of France's far-off sea.
Hurrying clouds, ships of the air,
would I could fly with you, sail everywhere,
salute the fair country where I was young.
I am a prisoner, fettered and chained,
and no ambassador have I to send.
But you may wander through the vaults of space:
no Queen of England holds you in this place.

Kennedy Oh dearest Lady! You are not yourself:
carried away by too much sudden freedom.

Mary Look, where the fisherman brings his ketch to shore:
that boat could bring my troubles to an end;
take me with speed where I could find a friend.

It is too evident the man is poor:
I shall load the boat with treasure,
more than his poor nets can measure,
quite beyond his imagination,
if he will bring me salvation.

Kennedy A hopeless dream. Can you not see that we
are still under surveillance from a distance?
A cruel prohibition scares away
any who might have shown you sympathy.

Mary Believe me, Hannah, it was not by chance
the prison doors were opened. This small favour
is herald of a greater happiness.
I know I'm not mistaken. And I have
to thank the hand of love for it. I trace
Lord Leicester's powerful hand in all of this.
They will enlarge the prison by degrees:
little by little letting me get used
to greater liberty, until at last
I see the man who will strike off my chains.

Kennedy I cannot understand these contradictions.
It was just yesterday you were condemned
to die, and now today this sudden freedom.
They say they also strike the chains off those
waiting to enter everlasting freedom.

[*Hunting horns in the distance*]

Mary Listen! The hunt. I can hear it quite clearly,
there in the distance. Sounding out loud.
If I could ride with them. Oh, I would dearly
love to be part of that great happy crowd.

[*Horns, nearer*]

Once more! That noise is so familiar.
What sweet, painful memories it calls forth.
How often would I hear it and rejoice,
swept onward by the hunters, while that voice
echoed across the Highlands of the North.

Paulet [*Entering*] Well, now, have I at last done something right?
Have I deserved your thanks, for once, my Lady?

Mary You, sir? Is it to you I owe this favour?
To you?

Paulet Why not to me? I was at court,
where I delivered what you gave to me –

Mary My letter? You delivered it? And is
this freedom which I now enjoy, is this
the consequence –

Paulet [*Pointedly*] And not the only one.
Prepare yourself for one of more importance.

Mary Of more importance, sir? What do you mean?

Paulet You hear the horns?

Mary [*Draws back in apprehension*]
You make me feel uneasy.

Paulet Her Majesty is riding with the hunt.

Mary No!

Paulet She will be here any minute.

Kennedy [*Hurrying to* MARY, *who is near to collapse*]
Lady!
What is the matter? You have turned quite pale.

Paulet Is something wrong? Is this not what you wanted?
Your wish is granted sooner than you thought.
You never used to be at a loss for words:
where are they now? Now is the time to speak!

Mary Oh, why was I not given any warning?
I'm not prepared for this, not now, not now.
What I had asked for, as the highest favour
now seems so frightening, so terrible:
come Hannah, take me back into the house,
till I regain some measure of composure.

Paulet Stay here. You must wait for her here. I see
quite clearly, that you are afraid
to stand before your judge, as well you might be.

Mary No, that is not the reason. Oh, my God,
this is another feeling. Shrewsbury,
Heaven has sent you as my guardian angel:
I cannot see her. Save me, save me from
the hated sight –

Shrewsbury [*Entering*] Madam, I beg you, summon all your courage:
this is the hour on which your fate depends.

Mary And for which I have waited, and prepared
myself for many years. I thought of everything
and memorised each way I'd try to move her,
and now that's suddenly all forgotten, all
wiped out and there is nothing left alive
in me, except a burning sense of wrong.
My heart is full of bloody hatred for her.
All my good thoughts have fled, and only fiends
stand around me, shaking out their Gorgon's hair.

Shrewsbury Calm your wild blood, control the bitterness
that's in your heart. No good can come of it,
when hatred meets with hatred. Obey the time
and circumstance, however much you feel
rebellion within. She holds the power.
You must abase yourself.

Mary To her? Never!

Shrewsbury You must!
Address her with due deference and composure.
Appeal to her benevolence, and do not,
not now, insist upon your rights. It's not the time.

Mary I called down my undoing on my head,
and by ill luck, my prayers have been answered.
We should never have set eyes on one another.
No good can come of it, not ever, never.
Fire will sooner fall in love with water,
the lamb will sooner lie down with the tiger.
I have tried too sorely, she has done
too much to hurt me, there can never be
a thought of mutual forgiveness.

Shrewsbury First
only meet her. I saw how deeply moved
your letter made her. Tears stood in her eyes.
She is not utterly devoid of feeling.
You need to trust her more yourself – that is
the reason why I have come on ahead;
to tell you what to do, and give you courage.

Mary [*Taking his hand*] Oh, Talbot, you have always been my friend.
If I could only have remained with you.
Things have gone hard with me since then.

Shrewsbury Forget
that now, only remember how to meet
the Queen with deference and humility.

Mary Is Burleigh with her too, my evil angel?

Shrewsbury No one is with her but the Earl of Leicester.

Mary Leicester!

Shrewsbury You need fear nothing from the Earl.
He does not wish your downfall. It was he
who finally induced the Queen to allow
this meeting.

Mary Ah! I knew it.

Shrewsbury What?

Paulet The Queen!

[*All stand aside. Only* MARY *remains, leaning on* KENNEDY*'s arm. The* QUEEN *enters, attended, with* LEICESTER]

Elizabeth What is that palace?

Leicester Fotheringay Castle.

Elizabeth [*To* SHREWSBURY] Send all the hunt ahead of us to London.
The populace is crawling in the streets.
We shall take refuge in this quiet park.

[SHREWSBURY *dismisses her train.* ELIZABETH *stares at* MARY, *while speaking to* LEICESTER]

My honest subjects love me all too well.
This uncontrolled idolatry would be
more suitable to a goddess than a mortal.

Mary [*Who has been leaning half-fainting, on* KENNEDY*'s arm, now rises and her eyes meet the tense gaze of* ELIZABETH. *She shudders, and throws herself again on her nurse's bosom*]
Dear God, that is a face without a heart.

Elizabeth Who is that lady?
[*General silence*]

Leicester Your Majesty, you are at Fotheringay.

Elizabeth [*Pretending astonishment, throwing an angry glance at* LEICESTER]
Which of you has done this? Lord Leicester? You?

Leicester Your Majesty, it is done. And now that Heaven
has guided your steps here, let noble pity
and magnanimity prevail.

Shrewsbury Your Majesty,
let us prevail on you to cast your eye
upon this most unhappy lady who
is overcome at sight of you.

[MARY *collects herself, and starts towards* ELIZABETH, *but stops halfway with a shudder, her features expressing a violent struggle*]

Elizabeth Well, Lords?
Which of you was it, then, described to me
a woman humbled, broken-spirited?
I find her proud, undaunted by misfortune.

Mary So be it. I'll submit to this as well:
shake off my impotent pride, try to forget
who I am, what I've suffered, and kneel down
to the woman who brought me to this disgrace.
[*She turns to* ELIZABETH]
Heaven has clearly favoured you, my sister,
awarded you the happy palm of victory;
I pay my homage to the God that raised you.
[*She falls at* ELIZABETH*'s feet*]
But now you too can show nobility.
Do not leave me lying here in shame;
give me your hand to raise me from the dust.

Elizabeth [*Steps back*] You are where you belong, my Lady Mary.
And I am thankful to God's grace, which would
not wish that I should lie there at your feet,
as you now lie at mine.

Mary [*With mounting emotion*]
Only consider
the mutability of human fortune.
There is a God who punishes our pride.
You should respect and fear that God of wrath
who casts me at your feet – in front of strangers.
You should respect me, and in me, respect
yourself, and not profane the Tudor blood
than runs in both our veins. Dear God in Heaven,
why must you stand there, like a rock, harsh, steep,
and inaccessible, on which the shipwrecked
castaway tries in vain to find a hold?
My life and fate hang on my words and tears.
Help me unlock my heart – let me move yours.

But when you freeze me with that icy stare,
a shudder closes up my heart, my tears
dry up, cold horror chokes my words up in my throat.

Elizabeth [*Cold, severe*] What was it that you wished to say to me?
You asked to speak to me. I shall ignore
the disrespect you show me as a Queen,
to do my duty as a sister should,
and offer you the comfort of my presence.
In following this generous impulse, I
expose myself to justified reproaches,
for lowering myself this far to you, since you
know very well you would have had me murdered.

Mary How am I to begin, how choose my words
so cleverly that they will touch your heart,
without offending it? God, take away
the sting from what I say, but leave the strength.
Whatever I can say on my own behalf
must accuse you, and that I do not want.
Your treatment of me has been wrong, since I
am just as much a Queen as you, and you
have held me prisoner. I came to you
for help, and you, in flagrant disregard
of all the laws of hospitality
and nations, threw me into prison. Friends
and servants were torn cruelly from me,
I was exposed to ignominious
privation, brought up on a trumped-up charge
before a court, illegally convened . . .
No more of that – let a veil be drawn
forever over what I suffered there.
Let us just say it was a twist of fate:
that you are not to blame, and nor am I.
An evil spirit rose from the abyss,
to foster mutual hatred in our hearts
from the beginning, even when we were children.
The hate grew up with us, and wicked men
fanned the ill-fated flame, while mad fanatics
put swords and daggers in unasked-for hands.
It is the cursed fate of kings that their disputes
divide the world, and let slip all the furies
of discord; but we need no longer speak
as strangers. We have met at last, as sisters.
[*Going to her trustingly, and speaking in a winning tone*]
Tell me now, sister, what was the wrong I did?

I want to give you fullest satisfaction.
Oh, had you only listened to me then,
when I tried so desperately to see you,
it never would have had to come to this;
this melancholy place would not have witnessed
this melancholy meeting.

Elizabeth My good angel
must have preserved me from nursing such a viper
in my bosom. No, it was not a twist
of fate, but your black heart, the wild ambition
of all your house, which is to blame for this.
There was no enmity between us, when
your uncle, that proud, power-hungry prelate
who stretches out his insolent hand toward
every crown, proclaimed his feud with me.
He hoodwinked you to taking on yourself
my coat of arms, my title to the crown,
and lastly, to take on myself, engage
in a struggle to the death – whom did he not
urge and incite to take up arms against me?
The tongues of priests, the swords of nations, and
the terrible weapons of religious frenzy;
but God is on my side, and that proud priest
is not yet master of the field: the blow
he aimed at my head, now will strike off yours.

Mary I am in God's hands. You would not abuse
your power so bloodily . . .

Elizabeth Who will prevent me?
Your uncle set a fine example how
kings can make peace with all their enemies.
The Massacre of Saint Bartholomew
shall be my model. What are the ties of blood,
the laws of nations, when the church can loose
all bonds of duty, sanctify betrayal,
and sanction regicide? I practise only
what your priests preach. On what security
might I now generously set you free?
What lock will keep your oath of loyalty
which can't be opened by St. Peter's keys?
The only real security is force;
I make no treaties with a brood of vipers.

Mary See the effects of your malign suspicion.
You've always looked upon me as a stranger,

an enemy. Had you named me your heir,
as is my right, my gratitude and love
would have made me your sister and your friend.

Elizabeth Abroad is where your friends are, Lady Stuart;
your family, the papacy; the monks,
your only brothers. I, name you my heir?
Machiavellian shifts! While I am still
alive, shall I allow you to seduce
my people, and embroil the noble youth
of all the kingdom in your harlotries –
until they all turn to the rising sun,
while I –

Mary Oh, rule in peace! I here renounce
all claims upon this kingdom. You have won.
I am the shadow of what once I was.
I have no more ambition, and the wings
that kept my spirit up are paralysed.
The long disgrace of prison has broken me.
You've done your worst, destroyed me in the flower
of youth – no, let us have an end of this.
Say what you came to say, for I cannot
believe you came here just to mock your victim.
Say it, just say to me: "Mary, you are free.
My power you have felt, now learn to feel
my magnamimity." Say this, and I'll accept
my life and freedom as a gift from you.
One word undoes all that has gone before.
I wait for it. Don't make me wait too long.
And woe betide you, Queen, if this is not
your final word. If you do not leave me
majestic, goddess-like, showering benefits –
Sister! I would not, for all this island,
for all the world, stand there before you as
you now stand before me.

Elizabeth Do you at last
admit defeat? Are all your intrigues over?
Have you no more assassins on their way?
No more adventurers to risk their necks
for you in yet another doomed excursion?
Yes, it is over, Lady Mary. You will turn
no more young heads. The world has other worries.
No one is eager to become your fourth
husband, since you seem to kill your suitors
much as you do your husbands.

Mary [*Flaring up*] Sister! Sister!
God grant me patience.

Elizabeth [*With a long look of haughty contempt*]
Do you see, Lord Leicester,
the charms no man could look on with impunity?
Next to which other women did not dare
to let themselves be seen? A reputation
of that sort can be cheaply gained. It costs
nothing at all, the beauty which is commonly
admired by all, is all too commonly
merely the beauty all have had in common.

Mary That is too much!

Elizabeth [*Laughs scornfully*]
Now you are showing us
your real face: it was a mask before.

Mary [*Blazing with anger, but speaking with dignity*]
I made mistakes, but I was young, and human;
power seduced me: I never denied
nor sought to hide the fact; with royal candour
I scorned to seem what I was not. The world
knows everything about me, and I say
that I am better than my reputation.
But what will you look like when they remove
the veil of virtue from your deeds, with which
you seek to cloak your . . . secret midnight lusts?
Virtue was not what you inherited
from Anne Boleyn: it is well known what virtue
finally brought your mother to the block.

Shrewsbury [*Stepping between them*]
Good God in Heaven! Must it come to this?
Lady Mary, is this moderation?
Is this submission?

Mary Moderation? I
have tolerated more than flesh and blood
can bear. Enough of patience, to the devil
with sweet submission, may my stifled anger
now break its chains, and burst out of its cage!
May he that gave the furious basilisk
its murderous stare, lay poison on my tongue . . .

[ELIZABETH *glares at* MARY, *speechless with fury*]

Shrewsbury She is beside herself. Forgive her madness.

Leicester [*In great agitation, trying to lead* ELIZABETH *away*]
You must not listen to a madwoman.
Come away now, from this unhappy place.

Mary A bastard has defiled the throne of England,
a noble-hearted nation is deceived
by a cunning cheat: if there were any justice
it would be you who should be lying here,
before me in the dust. I am your King!

[ELIZABETH *leaves quickly. The* LORDS *follow in deep perturbation*]

Kennedy What have you done? She left in such a fury.
Now all is over; there is no more hope.

Mary [*Still beside herself*]
She carries death with her. Hannah, at last,
[*Throwing her arms round* KENNEDY*'s neck*]
after the suffering, the degradation
a moment of revenge, of triumph! It's
as if a stone had fallen from my heart,
I've plunged a knife into my enemy's breast.

Kennedy She never will forgive the wound you gave her.
She is the Queen: she hurls the thunderbolts.
And you insulted her before her lover.

Mary Yes, I degraded her in Leicester's eyes.
He saw me do it, saw my victory,
the way I pulled her off her pedestal;
and he was there, his presence gave me strength.

[MORTIMER *enters*]

Kennedy Oh, sir, a terrible . . .

Mortimer I heard it all.
[*He gives* KENNEDY *a sign to go to her post, then comes closer, his whole being expressing violent passion*]
You won. You trod her in the dust. You were
the Queen, and she the criminal. I was
in wonder at your courage. You are a goddess,
and at this moment, I could worship you.

Mary You spoke to Leicester, you gave him my letter,
my present – tell me, sir . . .

Mortimer [*Looks at her with blazing eyes*]
Your noble anger

flamed round you, and transfigured all your charms.
You are the loveliest woman in the world.

Mary I beg you, sir, don't leave me in suspense.
What does my Lord say? Tell me what I may hope.

Mortimer Who? Leicester? He's a chicken-hearted coward.
There's no hope there. Despise him, and forget him.

Mary What are you saying?

Mortimer Is he the man to save you?
And to possess you? Let him dare to try.
He'll have to do so over my dead body.

Mary So you did not deliver him my letter?
Then I am lost.

Mortimer The coward loves his life.
The man who would deliver you, and make
you his, must know how he must welcome death.

Mary Will he do nothing then?

Mortimer Enough of him!
What can he do? What do we need from him?
I, and I alone, will rescue you

Mary Ah, what can you do?

Mortimer Do not deceive yourself,
your case is greatly changed since yesterday.
The mood in which the Queen left you just now,
the way the audience ended, has blocked all
the avenues of mercy. Now's the time
for action: boldness must decide. Chance all
if you would win all. But you must be free
before tomorrow's dawn.

Mary What do you say?
Before tomorrow. How can that be possible?

Mortimer Listen to the plan. Our friends are here,
convened together in a secret chapel,
where we have made confession to a priest
who has absolved us of all sins committed
and granted plenary remission of
all sins to be committed in the future.
We have received the final sacrament,
and now are ready for our final journey.

Mary Oh, God! What fearful preparation.

Mortimer Tonight we scale the castle walls. The keys
are in my hands. The guards will all be murdered;
you will be taken from your cell by force.
Nobody must be left behind alive,
no living soul who might betray us later.

Mary The wardens of my prison?

Mortimer They die first.

Mary Your uncle? He has been a father to you.

Mortimer He dies, and by my hand.

Mary A sin of blood.

Mortimer Our sins have been forgiven in advance.
I am free to do the worst, and I will do it.

Mary Oh, horrible, most horrible!

Mortimer If I must
murder the Queen herself, I shall not hesitate.
I swore it on the Body of Our Lord.

Mary No, Mortimer. Not all this blood for me –

Mortimer What is the meaning of all life to me
against my love for you? Oh, let the world
crumble in atoms, let a second deluge
swallow up all creation in its waves.
I care for nothing more. I shall not leave you.
If I am ever guilty of that crime,
God shall announce the brazen death of time.

Mary [*Recoils*] Oh, God, the way you talk, the way you look –
you frighten me; I cannot listen to you.

Mortimer [*With a distracted look, speaking in a tone of quiet madness*]
Life's but a span, and death is but a moment.
Let me be dragged to Tyburn, let me be
torn with red hot pincers, limb from limb,
so I may hold you in my arms, my love.
[*Approaching in great excitement, his arms spread wide*]

Mary [*Steps back*] Madman!
Don't touch me, sir, allow me to withdraw.

Mortimer All men are mad who cannot hold the joy
that's given them by God, fast in their arms.
Were it to cost a thousand lives, I'd save you.
And I shall save you, that I swear, but swear
by the living God, that I shall have you too.

Mary Is there no God, no angel to defend me?
How cruelly my fearful destiny
hurls me from one misfortune to another.
Was I born merely to awake such furies?
Have love and hate conspired to terrify me?

Mortimer I love you with the same power as they hate you.
They would behead you, they would have your neck,
so white, so dazzling, severed by the axe.
But offer willingly to the God of love
and life, what they would make you give to death.
Your beauty is no longer yours, make use
of it to give a lover happiness.
This hair already is the property
of death, use it to chain a willing slave.

Mary What must I hear, sir? Moderate your tone.
At least respect my grief, if not my rank.

Mortimer The crown has fallen from your head; the state
of earthly majesty's no longer yours.
Raise your voice in command, see if a friend
or servant comes to help you. You are nothing,
nothing except a lovely, tender woman,
the power of beauty, exquisite, divine,
which moves me to dare all and perform all,
which drives me headlong to the headsman's block –

Mary Oh, is there no one who will save me from him?

Mortimer Desperate service claims a like reward.
Why does a brave man shed his blood? Is not
the crown of life the living of it? He
would be a madman who threw it away.
First let me take you –

[*He seizes her in a violent embrace*]

Mary Must I call for help
against the man who came to save me?

Mortimer You
are not unfeeling, nor are you accused
of coldness by the world: your heart is known
to be not inaccessible to love.
You gave yourself to Rizzio, the singer,
and let that Bothwell treat you as he pleased.

Mary How dare you?

Mortimer He was nothing but your tyrant.
You worshipped him, for all he made you shudder.
He made you tremble, and not just with fear.
If it is fear you need to make you love,
by all the Gods of hell –

Mary Leave me. You're mad.

Mortimer I'll make you fear me as you once feared him.

Kennedy [*Bursting in*] They're here. They're coming. The whole park is filled
with soldiers.

Mortimer [*Starting up and reaching for his sword*]
Never fear, I shall defend you.

[*Enter* PAULET *and* DRURY *in great excitement.* ATTENDANTS *run across the stage*]

Mary Oh, Hannah, save me from this madman. Can
I find no refuge anywhere at all?
What saints must I invoke to intercede?
Violence is here, and murder waits within.

Paulet Lock all the gates and pull the drawbridge up.

Mortimer What is the matter, Uncle?

Paulet Where is she?
Where is the intriguing murderess?
Lock her away, for ever.

Mortimer What has happened?

Paulet It is the Queen.

Mortimer The Queen?

Paulet The Queen of England:
assassinated on the way to London!

Mortimer Am I delirious? Did someone say
the Queen had been assassinated? No,
no, I must be dreaming, in a fever,
which make the horrors in my mind seem true.
Who's that? O'Kelly! He looks terrified.

O'Kelly [*Bursting in*] Run, Mortimer, run! Everything is lost!

Mortimer Lost? What do you mean?

O'Kelly Don't waste time asking questions!
Just think how to escape.

Mortimer What is the matter?

O'Kelly It was Sauvage, the madman, struck the blow.

Mortimer It's true then?

O'Kelly Oh, it's true. Now save yourself!

Mortimer She's dead, and Mary will be Queen of England.

O'Kelly Dead? Who said so?

Mortimer You did.

O'Kelly She is alive!

Mortimer Alive?

O'Kelly It's you and I, and all of us, are dead.
The knife caught in her cloak, glanced off her.
Talbot disarmed the assailant.

Mortimer She is alive!

O'Kelly Alive to kill us all.
Come on, they'll have the park surrounded soon.

Mortimer What madman did this, though?

O'Kelly The Barnabite
from Toulon, you saw brooding in the chapel,
while the monk read out the Anathema
His Holiness pronounced upon Elizabeth.
He meant to take the shortest, easiest way,
at one fell swoop to free the Church of God,
and earn himself a martyr's crown. He told
nobody but the priest of his intentions,
and seized his chance, there, on the London road.

Mortimer And you, poor woman, what a cruel fate
pursues you. Now is the moment you should die;
your guardian angel has contrived your fall.

O'Kelly Tell me, where will you go? I'm going to hide
up North somewhere, in the woods.

Mortimer God be your guide!
I shall remain, and make one last attempt to save
the Queen of Scots, or find, with her, our common grave.

[*They run off in opposite directions*]

Act 4

Scene 1

[*An antechamber*]

Aubespine How is it with Her Majesty? My Lords,
you see me still beside myself with shock.
How was it possible? How could it happen
there, in the midst of all her loyal subjects?

Leicester It was no subject of Her Majesty's
that did it, but a subject of your King,
a Frenchman.

Aubespine And a madman, to be sure.

Kent No, no, Count Aubespine, it was a Papist.

[BURLEIGH *enters in conversation with* DAVISON]

Burleigh I want the death-warrant drawn up and sealed
immediately – when it is ready, it
will be taken to the Queen for signature.
Go now, we have no time to lose.

Davison My Lord.

[*He goes out*]

Aubespine [*Going to* BURLEIGH]
My Lords, I do sincerely share the joy
the nation feels, and rightly. God be praised
who kept the death-blow from her royal head!

Burleigh Praise Him for putting our enemies plots to shame!

Aubespine His judgment on the man who did this thing!

Burleigh The man who did it, and the villain who planned it.

Aubespine [*To* KENT]
Lord Marshal, would Your Lordship please conduct me
to audience with the Queen? I must convey
my Lord and Master's warm congratulations.

Burleigh You need not trouble yourself, Count Aubespine.

Aubespine [*Formal*] I think, Lord Burleigh, that I know my duty.

Burleigh Your duty is to make all speed you can
to leave this island now.

Aubespine [*Stepping back in amazement*]
What did you say?

Burleigh Diplomatic immunity protects you
today, but not tomorrow.

Aubespine May I ask
what is my crime?

Burleigh If I gave it a name
it could not be forgiven.

Aubespine Well, my Lord
I hope my right as an ambassador –

Burleigh – does not protect a traitor.

Leicester/Kent What was that?

Aubespine My Lord, consider well –

Burleigh A passport, signed
by you was found in the assassin's pocket.

Kent Is it possible?

Aubespine I issue many passports:
I cannot look into a person's thoughts.

Burleigh The murderer went to your house to confession.

Aubespine My house is open.

Burleigh To all enemies
of England.

Aubespine I demand investigation.

Burleigh I should beware of one.

Aubespine My sovereign is
insulted in my person. He will tear up
the treaty.

Burleigh Her Majesty has already done so.
England will not ally herself with France.
My Lord of Kent! You will please undertake
to give the Count safe-conduct to the sea.
The angry mob have stormed his palace, where
they found a veritable arsenal
of weapons – they are threatening to tear him

limb from limb if he shows his face. So hide him,
until their rage abates. You answer for
his life!

Aubespine Then I shall leave, yes, leave this country
where nation's rights are trodden underfoot
and treaties treated as toys – but my King
will call you to account –

Burleigh Just let him try!

[KENT *and* AUBESPINE *go out*]

Leicester So you are now dissolving the alliance
you took such pains to forge. You have deserved
scant thanks from England: might you not have saved
yourself the trouble?

Burleigh It seemed a good idea.
God wished it otherwise. Happy the man
who has no worse a burden on his conscience.

Leicester We know Lord Burleigh's dark, mysterious looks,
when he is ferreting out a crime of state.
My Lord, this is a happy time for you:
a hideous offence has been committed,
but by whom still remains a mystery.
There will be a tribunal of inquiry,
words will be weighed, and looks, and even thoughts
will come before the court. And you will be
the man of the hour, the Atlas of the state,
on whose broad back the whole of England rests.

Burleigh My Lord, in you I recognise my master.
For such a victory as your oratory
has won, I never could have done by mine.

Leicester And what, my Lord, is that supposed to mean?

Burleigh Was it not you who went behind my back
to lure the Queen to Castle Fotheringay?

Leicester Behind your back? When could my actions not
afford to be seen by you?

Burleigh You mean the Queen
took you to Fotheringay? I understand.
Did she indeed? It was not you who took
the Queen there, it was she who was obliging
enough to take you there. Now I see.

Leicester Just what is it you are trying to say, my Lord?

Burleigh You had her play a most distinguished role:
created quite a triumph for her too,
good, trusting, unsuspecting princess; she
was shamelessly and insolently mocked,
then ruthlessly betrayed and sacrificed.
Was that the mildness, the benevolence
which overcame you suddenly in council?
I take it this is why you found the Stuart
a contemptible, weak enemy, not worth
the trouble it would take to shed her blood.
Most elegant. I appreciate the point.
A point too fine to use: it breaks. How sad.

Leicester Sir, that is infamous. Please follow me;
explain yourself before Her Majesty.

Burleigh You'll find me there – and take good care, my Lord,
your eloquence does not desert you there.

[*Exit*]

Leicester I am discovered, he has seen through me.
How did that bloodhound happen on my track?
Does he have proof? If once the Queen discovers
the understanding between me and Mary,
what sort of guilty figure will I cut
in front of her? How sly and treacherous
my advice appears, and my unfortunate
attempt to bring the Queen to Fotheringay.
She sees I've made a cruel butt of her,
betrayed her to her hated enemy.
It will all seem to be premeditated:
even the bitter ending of the meeting,
her enemy's triumph, and her mocking laugh,
even the murderer's hand, a bloody horror.
that unexpected, monstrous stroke of fate
that intervened, she'll think was armed by me.
I see no help, nor hope at all. Who's here?

Mortimer [*Entering in extreme excitement, looking anxiously about him*]
Lord Leicester, is that you? Are we alone?

Leicester Not here, you wretched creature, what do you want?

Mortimer They're on our track, yours too; take care, my Lord.

Leicester Go! Go away!

Mortimer They know there was a secret
meeting at Count Aubespine's.

Leicester Why should
I care?

Mortimer They also know that the assassin
was present at it.

Leicester That is your affair!
What do you mean, presuming to enmesh me
in your insufferable bloody crimes?
Go and take care of your own vicious business.

Mortimer Only hear me, my Lord . . .

Leicester [*In violent anger*]
Go to the devil!
What are you doing clinging to my heels,
an evil genius? Go! I do not know you.
I have nothing in common with assassins.

Mortimer You will not listen to me. I have come
to tell you that you too have been betrayed.
The Lord High Treasurer was at Fotheringay.
Immediately the incident occured,
he had the Queen's apartments ransacked, and
they found there . . .

Leicester What?

Mortimer The first draft of a letter
addressed to you . . .

Leicester What was she thinking of?

Mortimer . . . in which she asks if you will keep your word,
renews her promise of her hand in marriage,
mentions the portrait which she sent . . .

Leicester Damnation!

Mortimer Lord Burleigh has the letter.

Leicester Then I <u>am</u> lost.

[*During* MORTIMER*'s next speech he paces up and down in despair*]

Mortimer Seize the moment: be ahead of it.
Anticipate him: seize your opportunity.
Save both yourself and her – swear you are innocent,
think of excuses, to prevent the worst.

I can do nothing more myself. I shall
escape to Scotland, find new allies there.
The affair is now in your hands: only try
what influence and a bold face can achieve.

Leicester [*Stopping still, suddenly self-possessed*]
I shall indeed. Guards! Here, arrest this traitor!
[*To the* OFFICER, *who enters with men-at-arms*]
Take him and guard him well. A plot has been
discovered. I shall inform the Queen myself.

[*Exit*]

Mortimer [*At first paralysed with astonishment, quickly collects himself, looking after* LEICESTER *with a look of deepest contempt*]
Villain! But it is what I deserve.
Why should I have trusted such a wretch?
My fall will be the bridge for his escape.
Save yourself, then – I shall not say a word.
I shall not implicate you in my ruin.
Even in death, I want no part of you.
Life is a wicked man's sole property.
[*To the officer of the guard, who comes forward to take him prisoner*]
What do you want, you slaves of tyranny?
I laugh at you, I am free, and my heart shall
freely express itself in its last moments.
[*He draws a dagger*]

Officer He has a weapon! Take away his dagger!

[*They crowd in on him; he defends himself*]

Mortimer Curses and ruin upon all of you
who have betrayed your God, and your true Queen,
who broke your faith with Mary, Queen on earth,
as you have done with Mary, Queen of Heaven,
and sold your honours to this royal bastard!

Officer You hear the blasphemy! Take him prisoner!

Mortimer My only love, I could not save your life,
then let me show you how a man can die.
Oh, Mary, Holy Mother, pray for me,
forgive me, and receive my soul on high.

[*He stabs himself, and falls into the arms of the guards*]

Scene 2

[*The* QUEEN*'s apartments*]

Elizabeth [*With a letter*]
So! I have been decoyed, and made a fool of!
The treachery, to lead me out in triumph
to meet his mistress! There has never been
so abject a betrayal of a woman.

Burleigh What I cannot yet understand is how
Your Majesty's sagacity was imposed on.

Elizabeth Oh, I could die of shame, to think how he
must have laughed at my weakness, standing there
thinking I was humiliating her,
while all the time I was her butt and scoff.

Burleigh Your Majesty will agree my advice was loyal.

Elizabeth Oh, yes, I have been punished cruelly
for straying from the straight path of your guidance.
But how could I not trust him? Why should I
suspect a snare in his true love for me?
Who can I trust, if he deceives me so?
The man I raised above the heads of all,
who always was the nearest to my heart,
whom I allowed to bear himself at court
as if he were the master, no – the King!

Burleigh And who was, at the same time, betraying you,
playing you false with the false Queen of Scotland.

Elizabeth And she will pay me for this with her blood.
Is the warrant ready?

Burleigh As you ordered.

Elizabeth She shall die, and he shall see her die,
then die himself. I have put a divorce
between my heart and him: there's no more love,
only revenge. High as he stood, his fall
will be as steep, and ignominious.
And as he was an example of my weakness
now he will be a monument to my strength.
Have him escorted to the Tower. I shall
name peers to be his judges. He shall be
exposed to the full rigour of the law.

Burleigh He will besiege you, try to justify –

Elizabeth How can he justify himself? Does not
the letter prove his guilt? His crime is clear.

Burleigh Nevertheless, your mild forgiving nature,
allied to his appearance, and his presence . . .

Elizabeth I will not see him. Never, never again.
Have you given order that he is
to be refused admittance if he comes?

Burleigh I have.

Page [*Entering*]
The Earl of Leicester!

Elizabeth Oh, the devil!
I do not wish to see him. Tell him that.

Page I would not dare to tell His Lordship that;
nor would he believe me if I did.

Elizabeth So this is how I raised him up! So that
my servants fear him more than they do me.

Burleigh [*To the* PAGE] The Queen forbids Lord Leicester to come in.

[*The* PAGE *goes out hesitantly*]

Elizabeth [*After a pause*]
And yet, it might be possible – what if
he had his reasons? Tell me, might it not
have been a stratagem of that woman
to separate me from my dearest friend?
She is a devil in the flesh. If she
had written that letter purposely to poison
my mind against a man she hates, and would
destroy . . .

Burleigh Your Majesty, consider carefully . . .

Leicester [*Opening the door violently and entering with
an imperious look*]
Where is the man who has the insolence
to bar me access to my sovereign?

Elizabeth How dare you!

Leicester Turning me away? If she
can be seen by Burleigh, so she can by me!

Burleigh You're very bold, my Lord, to burst in here
without permission.

Leicester And you, my Lord, are very impudent.
Permission? There is no one here at court
who grants me or refuses me permission.
[*Approaching* ELIZABETH *humbly*]
I wish to hear it from my Queen's own lips . . .

Elizabeth [*Turning away*] Out of my sight! you are contemptible.

Leicester I do not recognise Elizabeth
in these harsh words. I recognise my enemy,
that Lord. But I rely on my Elizabeth.
You have heard him. Now I demand the same.

Elizabeth Speak then. Increase your perfidy by denial.

Leicester First let this troublesome importunate
withdraw – take yourself off, my Lord – there is
no need for witnesses for what I have
to say to the Queen. Go!

Elizabeth Stay! That is an order.

Leicester Between us there is no need of third parties.
My business is with my Gloriana,
and no one else – I stand upon the rights
of my position – sacred rights indeed,
and I insist my Lord here takes his leave.

Elizabeth This hectoring tone is most appropriate.

Leicester It is indeed. I am the man whom your
preferment gave pre-eminence above
him and all others. It was your heart gave me
my high position, as a gift of love.
I shall maintain it though it should cost my life.
Let him go – and we shall not need more
than two brief moments to reach an agreement.

Elizabeth You are mistaken, sir, if you imagine
you can get round me with such tricks.

Leicester The one
who has got round you is that chatterbox.
I want to speak directly to your heart;
and what I dared to do, trusting your favour.
I only want to justify before
your heart – I recognise no other court
than your affection.

Elizabeth Have you so little shame,
you can appeal to what you've most betrayed?
My Lord, show him the letter.

Burleigh Here it is.

Leicester [*Glancing at the letter with no sign of unease*]
This is the Queen of Scotland's hand.

Elizabeth Read and say nothing.

Leicester [*Calmly, after he has finished reading*]
Appearances may be against me, but
in spite of all appearances, I hope
appearances are not what I'll be judged by.

Elizabeth Can you deny that you negotiated
in secret with the Lady Stuart, that you
received her portrait, and led her to hope
that you would set her free?

Leicester It would be easy,
did I have guilty feelings, to dismiss
the statement of an enemy; but I do not
have anything on my conscience; I admit
what she writes is the truth.

Elizabeth You miserable wretch.

Burleigh Self-condemned.

Elizabeth Now get out of my sight.
To the Tower with you – traitor.

Leicester That I am not.
It was an error not to tell you of
this step, but my intentions were impeccable:
to scout the enemy's plans, and then to scotch them.

Elizabeth Feeble excuses.

Burleigh My Lord, do you think –

Leicester I played a dangerous game, and only Leicester,
of all the men at court, could dare to play it.
All the world knows I hate the Queen of Scots.
The rank I hold, the trust with which the Queen
delights to honour me, sweeps every doubt
of my true end aside. The man whom you
so singled out for greatness, surely he
may blaze his own bold trail to do his duty.

Burleigh Why keep such worthy aspirations secret?

Leicester [*Looking at him with contempt*]
My Lord, your practice is to talk before
you act, to be your own advertisement.
That may be well for you, my Lord, but I
prefer to act first and talk afterwards.

Burleigh And what prompts your loquacity at present?

Leicester You may congratulate yourself on your success,
as no doubt you are doing: you have saved
the Queen, unmasked a treasonous plot; you think
nothing escapes your beady eye and fine
intelligence. You miserable braggart!
In spite of all your rummaging, but for me
the Queen of Scotland would be free today.

Burleigh How can you say . . ?

Leicester With ease, my Lord. The Queen
took Mortimer into her confidence;
her deepest confidence, indeed she went
so far as to propose a bloody mission
against the Queen of Scots, the same proposal
his uncle had rejected with disdain.
Did she or did she not?

Burleigh [ELIZABETH *and* BURLEIGH *look at one onother, dismayed*]
How do you reach
that quaint conclusion?

Leicester Did she or did she not?
Well, now, my Lord, where were your thousand eyes,
that you should fail to see that Mortimer
had tricked you, that he was Queen Mary's creature,
a rabid papist, instrument of the Guise,
a bold fanatic who had come to free
the Queen of Scots and kill the Queen of –

Elizabeth [*Utterly astonished*]
Mortimer!

Leicester The go-between, through whom Mary Stuart
negotiated with me; that is how I met him.
And she should, this very day have been
set free. He has just told me so himself.
I ordered his arrest, and in despair
at seeing his work frustrated, him unmasked,
he killed himself.

Elizabeth Such treason is unheard of!
That Mortimer!

Burleigh And this took place just now?
After I left you?

Leicester For my own part, I
must very much regret it had to end
like that. His testimony, were he still
alive, would have exonerated me
completely, and removed all trace of guilt.
That was the reason why I handed him
over to the judges – so the strict
process of law might prove my innocence
before the world.

Burleigh He killed himself, you said?
Or did you kill him?

Leicester That's a filthy slander!
Question the guard I summoned to arrest him.
[*He goes to the door and calls outside. The* OFFICER *of the guard enters*]

Inform Her Majesty how Mortimer
came by his death.

Officer I was on duty in
the antechamber, when the door was thrown
open by my Lord, who ordered me
to arrest the knight on charges of High Treason.
At which, we saw him fly into a rage,
pull out a dagger, with a violent curse
upon Her Majesty. Before we could
prevent him, he had plunged it in his heart
and fallen to the floor, dead.

Leicester That will do.
You may withdraw. The Queen has heard enough.

[*The* OFFICER *goes out*]

Elizabeth Oh, what a bottomless pit of infamy!

Leicester Now who was it saved you? My Lord Burleigh?
Did he know what dangers threatened you?
Did he turn them aside? Your faithful Leicester
was your good angel.

Burleigh Mortimer's death was not
inopportune for you, my Lord.

Elizabeth I know not what to say,
I do believe you, and yet not believe you.
I see in you both guilt and innocence.
Oh, that woman! To make me feel such pain!

Leicester Then she must die. I vote now for her death.
I formerly advised the sentence be
suspended till another arm was raised
for her – it has been – and I now demand
immediate execution of the sentence.

Burleigh You advised that, my Lord?

Leicester Much as it may
appal me to proceed to such extremes,
I now see and believe, the welfare of
Her Majesty demands this sacrifice;
I submit, therefore, that the death-warrant
be drawn up with no more delay.

Burleigh And I submit,
seeing my Lord's devotion and sincerity,
that he be charged with carrying out the warrant.

Leicester I should be?

Burleigh You. What better way to lull
any suspicions that still linger over you,
than supervising the beheading of
the woman with whom, or so your enemies say,
you were in love?

Elizabeth Sterling advice, my Lord!
So be it, then.

Leicester I would have thought my rank
would have exempted me from duties of
so ominous a kind. In every way it would
more suit a man like Burleigh than myself.
Standing as close as I do to the Queen,
I should not be concerned in such grim work.
Nevertheless, I shall display my zeal:
if it will satisfy my sovereign,
I shall forgo the privilege of my rank
to undertake this most repugnant duty.

Elizabeth Burleigh shall share it with you. [*To* BURLEIGH] See to it;
the warrant must be drawn up instantly.

[BURLEIGH *goes out. Clamour outside*]

What is that noise? What is the meaning of
this uproar in the street? What is it, Kent?

Kent [*Enters*] Your Majesty, the mob surrounds the palace,
clamouring frantically to see you.

Elizabeth What
do my people want?

Kent The city is alarmed;
they say your life is threatened, that assassins
sent by the Vatican are everywhere.
The Catholics are rumoured to have plotted
to snatch the Queen of Scotland from her prison,
and crown her Queen in London. This is what
the populace believes, and they are frantic.
Nothing will pacify them but the head
of Mary Stuart, and that must be off today.

Elizabeth What? Would they force me?

Kent They are quite determined;
they will not leave till you have signed the warrant.

[*Renter* BURLEIGH, *with* DAVISON *with a document*]

Elizabeth What do you have there? Davison?

Davison [*Approaches gravely*]
Your Majesty
required me to –

Elizabeth What is it?
[*About to take the paper, she recoils*]
Oh, my God.

Burleigh The voice of the people is the voice of God,
obey it.

Elizabeth [*Struggling with her indecision*]
Oh, my Lords. Who is it can tell me
whether or not this is the voice of all
my people, of the world, which I can hear?
I deeply fear that once I have obeyed
the wishes of the mob, that quite another
voice will be heard – and that those very men
who now impel me forcibly to act,
will be the first to blame me when I have done.

Shrewsbury [*Enters, much disturbed*]
They would force you to over-hasty action.
Your Majesty, be firm, do not give in . . .
[*Sees* DAVISON *with the document*]
Or is it done already? I can see
an inauspicious paper in your hand:
it must not be presented to the Queen –
the Queen must not be shown it.

Elizabeth My Lord Talbot,
they force me.

Shrewsbury Who is it can force you here?
Are you the Queen? Then show them that you are.
Command those raucous voices to be silent,
that have the impudence to force your will
and try to influence the sovereign's judgment.
Nor are you now yourself, you are only human,
and too vexed now to make an impartial judgment.

Burleigh The judgment has been made some time ago.
Sentence is not to be pronounced, but carried out.

Kent [*Who had left at* SHREWSBURY*'s entrance, now returns*]
The uproar's getting worse, the mob is not
going to be held in check much longer.

Elizabeth You see how they beset me.

Shrewsbury All I ask for
is delay. This one stroke of the pen
decides your peace of mind and happiness
for life. You've thought of this for years –
shall a moment's haste carry you past recall?
Only a short delay. Compose yourself,
wait for a quieter time.

Burleigh [*Angry*] Await, delay,
hesitate, until the kingdom is
in flames around us, and the enemy
finally succeeds in carrying out
her murderous intentions. Three times now
God's turned aside the blade; today it missed
you by a hair's breadth: it is tempting God
to hope for yet another miracle.

Shrewsbury The God, whose wonder-working hand has saved
you four times now, and given an old man
the strength to overpower a fanatic –

deserves your trust. I shall not now set forth
the claims of justice: now is not the time:
that storm out there makes them inaudible.
Only hear this: you fear the living Mary.
It is the dead, beheaded Mary you
should fear. She will rise from her grave to haunt
all England, a goddess of revenge and discord,
who'll turn your people's hearts away from you.
The English hate her now, because they fear her;
but once she is no more, they will avenge her,
seeing in her no longer any threat
to their religion, only seeing her
the grandchild of their kings, the victim of
hatred and persecution. You will soon
experience the change. Just ride through London
once the bloody deed has taken place;
show yourself to the people who have always
crowded about you, cheering and you'll see
another England, and another people.
You will no longer be surrounded by
the halo of justice which has won all hearts.
Terror, the tyrant's grisly companion,
will stalk before you shuddering, and lay waste
the streets through which you pass. You will be guilty
of the worst crime in the world: what head is safe
if that of God's anointed is struck off?

Elizabeth Talbot, you saved my life today; you turned
the assassin's knife aside – oh, why did you
not let it strike? These conflicts would be over:
I should be free from doubt, and clear from blame,
lying in my quiet grave. I am so weary
of life and crown: if one of us must die
– and I can see there is no other way –
to let the other live, can I not be
the one who gives way? Let the people choose.
I will give up my sovereignty. God is
my witness that I always lived for them.
Not for myself.
If they can hope for happier days with her,
the Stuart, the flatterer, the younger queen,
I shall be happy to resign the throne,
and to withdraw to Woodstock, where I spent
my unambitious youth, in solitude,

and where, removed from all the worldly lures
of greatness, I found greatness in myself.
I was not framed to rule. A ruler must
know how to be hard: my heart is soft.
I have ruled this island long and happily
because I only had to bring it happiness.
My first hard royal duty has revealed
my impotence.

Burleigh Now, by God's blood and bones,
if I must listen to such words, unworthy
of a monarch, issuing from a monarch's lips,
I should betray my duty and my country
if I kept silent any longer. – You
say that, more than yourself, you love your people.
Then prove it. Do not choose peace for yourself,
and leave your country to be racked with tempests.
Think of the church! Shall the old superstition
come back here with the Stuarts? Shall the monks
rule here again, the papal legate come
from Rome to close our churches, and dethrone
our kings? The saving or damnation of
the souls of every subject of this land
depends on how you act, and now. This is
no time for weakness or prevarication.
The people's welfare is your first concern.
Talbot has saved your life, but I shall save
England! Which is more.

Elizabeth Leave me to my
own thoughts. There is no human aid nor comfort
to be expected in this weighty business.
I shall submit it to a higher judge.
And what he teaches me, I shall perform.
You may withdraw, my Lords, [*To* DAVISON] You will remain.

[*The* LORDS *go out. Only* SHREWSBURY *remains for a moment standing before the* QUEEN, *looking at her with meaning, then he too slowly goes out, with an expression of profound sadness*]

The slavery of service to the people!
Humiliating servitude! How tired I am
of flattering an idol I despise!
When shall this head that wears a crown lie easy?
Defer to their opinions? Fawn on them

for praise, a stinking mob who would prefer
to clap a mountebank? No one's a king
who still must please the world, but only he
who need not ask for any man's approval.
I've practised justice, scorned the arbitrary
ways of tyrants all my life, and why?
Only to find, the moment violence is
inevitable, that my hands are tied.
The example that I gave myself condemns me.
Were I a tyrant like my elder sister
Mary, my predecessor on my throne,
I could shed royal blood without a voice
being raised in criticism. But did I
make the choice of justice willingly?
Necessity, which sways the will of kings,
can sometimes prompt a virtuous decision.
I am surrounded by my enemies;
only my people's love preserves my crown.
The Continental powers conspire my ruin:
the Pope hurles down anathema on my head:
France has betrayed me with the Judas kiss
of brotherhood, and out to sea, the Spaniard
wages an open fierce war of destruction.
So here I stand, a weak, defenceless woman,
fighting against a world in arms. I must
cover the nakedness of my claim with virtues,
conceal the blemish which my father gave me
at birth – faint hope of that! – the malice of
my enemies strips me bare, confronts me with
that eternal threatening spectre, Mary Stuart.
This fear must have an end. Her head shall fall.
I shall have peace. She is my nemesis.
Wherever I have planted joy or hope,
I find this snake of hell across my path.
She tears my lover from me, steals my bridegroom.
All the disasters that bedevil me
are all called MARY STUART. Once she is dead
I shall be free as the air upon the mountains.
The scorn as her glance fell on me, as if
the lightning should have struck me where I stood.
But she is powerless, I have the better weapons.
One fatal stroke and you will be no more.
[*Goes quickly to the table and seizes the pen*]
You call me bastard, you unhappy wretch?

I am one only while you live and breathe.
All doubt surrounding my own royal birth
will disappear the moment you do too.
The bed where I was born becomes legitimate,
the moment England can no longer choose between us.
[*She signs, quickly and firmly, then drops the pen, and recoils with a frightened expression. After a pause, she rings a bell.* DAVISON *enters*]

Elizabeth Where are the other lords?

Davison They have all gone
to call the mob to order. They became
quiet the moment Shrewsbury appeared.
"He is the one" a hundred voices shouted,
"He is the one. The man who saved the Queen!
Listen to him. The bravest man in England."
Then Talbot spoke, gently reproving them
for their recourse to violence, with such conviction
that they were pacified and slunk away
in silence.

Elizabeth They will change with every wind.
I pity the man who leans on that weak reed.
Thank you, Sir William, you may leave us now.
[*He turns to go*]
Oh, and this paper – take it back – I give
it back to you.

Davison [*Looks at the paper, startled*]
Madam! Your signature?
Your Majesty has decided?

Elizabeth I was asked
to sign this. I have done so. But a piece
of paper decides nothing. Names don't kill.

Davison Your name, Your Majesty, upon this piece
of paper will do both, a thunderbolt
on lethal wings. This document commands
the sheriff and the Lords Commissioners
to go at once to Fotheringay Castle,
to inform the Queen of Scots she is to die
and to see it done without delay by dawn
The moment that this paper leaves my hands,
her life is over.

Elizabeth Yes, sir, God has laid
a mighty destiny in your weak hands.
Pray that He may give you enlightenment.
I leave you to your duty.
[*Turns to go*]

Davison [*Blocking her*] No, Your Majesty.
Do not abandon me before you have
enlightened me. Or is there any further
enlightenment required except that I
should follow your requirements, to the letter?
You place the paper in my hand in order that
I should discharge its contents with despatch?

Elizabeth That I leave to your own intelligence.

Davison Not mine! Heaven forfend! Intelligence
for me is indistinguishable from
obedience. Your servant should not have
to undertake decisions in this business.
The slightest slip here would be regicide,
incalculable, terrible disaster.
Allow me merely to be your instrument
with neither eyes, nor mind, nor will in this.
Tell me your meaning unequivocally:
what is to happen to this death warrant?

Elizabeth The name says what it means.

Davison But does that mean
you that desire its instant execution?

Elizabeth I did not say so, but the thought of it
makes me shudder.

Davison Then you would have me keep it
until some later time?

Elizabeth [*Quickly*] At your own risk.
Upon your own head be the consequences.

Davison Mine? God! Your Majesty, what do you want?

Elizabeth [*Impatient*] I want an end to this whole wretched business.
Want it forgotten, want it no more thought of,
want to be free of it, now and forever.

Davison One single word is all that it would cost you.
Speak it, and tell me what I must do with this?

Elizabeth I have said it, now do not plague me further.

Davison Said it? But you have said nothing to me.
Oh, may it please the Queen to bear in mind . . .

Elizabeth [*Stamps her foot*]
Intolerable!

Davison Have patience with your servant.
I have only held this office a few months.
The speech of Kings and courts is still a foreign
language to me. Where I grew up, our ways
were plain, our customs simpler. Please have patience.
Do not be niggard of the word which tells me
clearly what is my duty.
[*He goes to her, pleadingly. She turns her back on him. He stands a moment in despair, then speaks in a determined tone*]
Take it back.
Your Majesty, take back the paper.
It is as if I held a burning coal.
Find someone else to be your go-between
in this appalling business.

Elizabeth Do your office.
[*She goes out*]

Davison She's gone. And left me with this warrant,
baffled and undecided – what am I
to do? Shall I retain it? Pass it on?
[*To* BURLEIGH, *who enters*]
Oh, good that you have come, my Lord. You were
the person who appointed me to office.
Release me from it now. I took it on
not knowing what it would entail. Let me
return to the obscurity from which
you took me. This is not the place for me.

Burleigh What ails you, sir? Come, pull yourself together.
Where is the warrant? What were the Queen's commands?

Davison She has just left me, in high anger. Oh, my Lord,
tell me what I must do. Deliver me
from this infernal doubt. Here is the warrant.
It has been signed.

Burleigh It has? Give it to me!
Give it to me.

Davison I dare not.

Burleigh What?

Davison The Queen
has not yet made it clear –

Burleigh Not clear? She signed.
Give it to me.

Davison I have to see that it
is carried out – or that it is not carried out.
What, in God's name am I to do?

Burleigh [*More urgently*] You are
to see that it is carried out at once.
Give it to me. Do not prevaricate
or you are lost.

Davison I'm lost if I do not.

Burleigh Your wits are clearly lost already, fool.
[*He seizes the paper, and hurries out*]
Give me that warrant.

Davison [*Running after him*]
What are you doing? Stop!
This is the end of everything for me.

Act 5

Scene 1

[*The scene is the same room as Act One*]

[HANNAH KENNEDY, *in deep mourning, her eyes red with weeping, with deep, quiet grief, is busy sealing packets and papers. Grief frequently interrupts her work, and every now and then she is seen to pray in silence*]

[*Enter* PAULET *and* DRURY, *also in black. They are followed by numerous servants carrying gold and silver vessels, mirrors, paintings and other valuable objects, with which they fill the rear part of the room.* PAULET *hands over to the* NURSE *a jewel-box, along with a paper, and signifies to her, by gestures, that it contains an inventory of the things being brought in. The sight of these treasures renews the* NURSE*'s grief. She sinks into a deep melancholy, as the others silently withdraw. Enter* MELVILLE. KENNEDY *cries out at the sight of him*]

Kennedy Melville, it's you! To see you once again!

Melville My good, loyal Kennedy, we meet once more.

Kennedy It's been a long and painful separation.

Melville This is a painful, sad reunion.

Kennedy Oh, God! You've come –

Melville To pay my last respects
and bid my Queen farewell for evermore.

Kennedy Finally, on the morning of her death
she is allowed to have the friends by her,
she was forbidden for so long. Oh, sir,
I shall not ask how things have been with you,
nor shall I burden you with an account
of all that we have suffered since the day
that you were torn from us – there will be time
enough, God knows, to speak of that. Oh, Melville,
why did we have to live to see this day?

Melville Let us not weaken one another with
our tears. As long as life is left to me
I'll mourn for her. I shall not smile again.

And all my life I shall wear black for her.
But now I shall be steadfast, and you too.
Promise me to moderate your grief –
and if the rest should give way to despair,
let us be strong, and worthy to precede her
and be her rod and staff to Calvary.

Melville Melville, you are mistaken if you think
the Queen needs our support. It will be she
who sets us an example of composure.
Do not fear. Mary Stuart will die a Queen.

Melville How did she receive the dreadful news?
They say that she was not prepared for it.

Kennedy No more she was. It was quite another fear
that terrified my Lady; not the fear
of death, but that of being liberated.
– Freedom had been promised us. This very night
Mortimer was to have arranged our flight.
The Queen was poised between her fear and hope,
and in some doubt whether she could entrust
her person and her honour to that boy.
She waited for the dawn. – When suddenly,
there was a tumult in the castle, sounds
of hammering assailed our ears, and knocking:
we thought that it must be our rescuers;
hope beckoned and the appetite for life
sprang up unbidden, overpoweringly –
Then a door opened – it was Paulet, saying
the carpenters were putting up the scaffold
right beneath our feet.

Melville Oh, gracious Heavens!
How did she bear the shock of this reverse
of fortune?

Kennedy [*After a pause in which she regains a degree of composure*]
Life is not a thing which one
leaves by degrees: there is a moment when
one has to cut the knot of time and turn
one's face towards eternity. In that moment
God granted her the strength to turn her back
with firm decision on all earthly hope,
and trust in Heaven. Not a sign of fear,
no word of weak lament disgraced my Lady.
Only when she heard of Leicester's treachery,

the cruel fate of Mortimer, when she saw
the misery of his old uncle, who had lost,
because of her, the last hope of his life:
only then did she weep. Not her own fate,
but someone else's grief, drew forth her tears.
The rest of the night she spent in prayer, and writing
last letters to her dearest friends, then with
her own hand she drew up her testament.
Now she is resting for a moment: her
last sleep will be refreshing . . .

Melville Who is with her?

Kennedy Burgoyne, her own physician, and her ladies.
[*Enter* MARGARET CURLE]
What is it, Margaret? Has my Lady woken?

Curle She's dressed already – and she's asking for you.

Kennedy I'll go to her.
[*To* MELVILLE, *who starts to go with her*]
No, do not follow me.
Wait till I have prepared her for your coming.
[*She goes out*]

Curle Melville – our old court steward!

Melville Yes, it is.

Curle We do not need a steward any more.
Melville, you came from London. Can you give
me any news what's happened to my husband?

Mlville They say he will be freed the moment that –

Curle The moment that the queen is dead. The worthless,
despicable traitor! He is the murderer of
our poor, dear Lady. They say it was his
testimony condemned her.

Melville Yes, it was.

Curle Then may his soul be damned to Hell for it!
He bore false witness –

Melville Lady Curle, please think
what you are saying.

Curle I would swear to it
in a court of law, yes, and I would repeat it
to his face, and proclaim it to the world
that she dies innocent –

Melville God grant she may!

Burgoyne [*Enters, sees* MELVILLE]
Melville!

Melville [*Embracing him*]
Burgoyne!

Burgoyne [*To* CURLE]
Take a glass of wine
to your mistress. Hurry!

Melville Is the Queen not well?

Burgoyne She thinks she is: her courage, though, deceives her
She thinks she needs no sustenance, but she
still has a heavy trial ahead of her.
Her enemies shall not boast it was the fear
of death that made her cheeks so pale, when it
was only natural weakness and fatigue.

Melville [*To* KENNEDY, *re-entering*]
Where is she now? Can you take me to her?
Will she see me?

Kennedy She will be coming soon.
You seem to look about you with amazement,
as if to ask me: what is all this splendour
in a house of death? We were deprived in life:
it took death to bring back this luxury.
[*Two more of* MARY'*s ladies-in-waiting enter, also in mourning. On seeing* MELVILLE *they burst into loud weeping*]

Melville Oh, what a sight! And what a meeting! Gertrude!
And Rosamund!

Second Lady She sent us out. She wants
to be alone with God for one last time.
[*Two maidservants enter, in black like the rest, expressing their grief with silent gestures. Enter* MARGARET CURLE, *carrying a gold cup of wine, which she puts on the table: pale and shaking, she holds on to a chair for support*]

Melville Madame, what is it? What has frightened you?

Curle Oh, God!

Burgoyne What is the matter?

Curle I have seen it.

Melville Collect yourself, and tell us what it was.

Curle I was coming with the wine up the main stairway
that leads down to the hall below – the door
was open – I glanced in – and saw – oh, God –

Melville Saw what?

Curle The walls all hung with black, and in the centre
a scaffold rose up, also hung with black,
and in the centre of the scaffold stood
the block, the cushion, black as well, and by them
there lay a shining, sharpened headman's axe –
The hall was full of people crowding round
the murderous thing, and in their eyes I saw
the hot desire for blood.

Melville Hush! Here she comes.

[*Enter* MARY. *She is dressed festively, in white, with a necklace of little beads, with an Agnus Dei hanging from it, a rosary at her waist, and a crucifix in her hand. She has a diadem in her hair, and her great black veil is thrown back. At her appearance, those present fall back on either side, expressing their violent sorrow.* MELVILLE, *with an involuntary movement, sinks to his knees.* MARY *surveys the whole gathering with quiet majesty*]

Mary Why do you grieve? Why do you weep? You should
be happy with me, now the end of grief
is finally in sight, now my chains fall,
my prison will open and my radiant soul
take flight on angel's wings to eternal freedom.
When I was in my arrogant enemy's power,
and suffering humiliation
unworthy of a free and sovereign Queen,
then was the time you should have wept for me.
– Death comes to me now, healing, comforting,
a stern, grave friend: he covers my dishonour
with his black wings. – However low we sink,
our death restores nobility to us.
I feel the crown once more upon my head,
and pride and dignity within myself.
[*She moves forward a few paces*]
What? Melville! – Do not kneel. Oh, rise, sir, rise.
You are present at my triumph, not my death.
I am more fortunate that I dared hope:
my reputation will no longer be
left to the mercy of my enemies,
now that I have one friend who shares my faith

to be a witness at my hour of death.
Tell me Sir, how you have fared since you were torn
from us, in this ungracious, hostile country?
My heart has often been concerned for you.

Melville I felt no want, except my grief for you,
that, and my inability to serve you.

Mary And Didier, my old chamberlain, how is he?
Oh, but that loyal old man must be long dead
by now, for he was very old.

Melville God has
not granted him that favour; he is still
alive, to see you buried in your youth.

Mary It would have been such happiness, before
I died, to kiss the faces of my family.
But I shall die among strangers, and your tears
will be the only ones I know are shed.
Melville, I entrust you with the carrying-out
of my last wishes – take my blessing to
my brother, the Most Christian King of France,
and all his house, the Cardinal, my uncle,
Henri de Guise, my noble cousin: also
the Pope, Christ's representative on earth;
may he be pleased to bless me in his turn:
and his Most Catholic Majesty, the King
of Spain, who nobly offered me his service
as rescuer and avenger. All their names
are mentioned in my will: however poor
the gifts I have bequeathed to them, as tokens
of my love to them they will not despise them.
[*Turning to her servants*]
You I have commended to the King
of France, my brother; he will care for you.
If my last wish means anything to you,
do not remain in England, do not let
the English cruelly gloat at your misfortunes,
seeing those in the dust who once served me.
Give me your oath upon the crucifix
to leave the land as soon as I am dead.

Melville I swear it in the name of all those here.

Mary Though poor and plundered, what I still possess
of which I have the free disposal, is
divided amongst you. Let us hope that they

will honour my last wishes. In addition
all that I wear on my last walk is yours.
Allow me one last taste of earthly pomp
as I go on my way to Heaven. [*To her women*] To you,
Alice, Gertrude, Rosamund, I leave
my pearls, and all my dresses: you are young,
and still take pleasure in such finery.
Margaret, you have far the greatest claim
upon my generosity, since you
are the unhappiest of all I leave
behind – my will shall show that I do not
take vengeance on you for your husband's guilt.
My faithful Hannah, gold and jewels mean nothing
to you: I think my memory will be
your greatest treasure. Take this scarf!
I have embroidered it with my own hands
for you in my long hours of misery.
My tears are woven into it. Please bind
my eyes with this scarf when the time shall come.
This last thing that is done for me I should
like to be done by you, my Hannah.

Kennedy Melville,
I cannot bear this.

Mary Come now, it is time.
Come nearer and receive my last farewell.
[*She holds out her hands: one after another, they fall at her feet, kissing her extended hands, weeping passionately*]
Margaret, farewell, and Alice, too:
Burgoyne, thank you for your devoted service:
Gertrude, how hot your lips are – I have been
much hated, but I have been much loved as well.
Gertrude, I hope you find a worthy husband;
your heart is warm, and needs the warmth of love.
Bertha! You have made the better choice,
to be the unsullied bride of Christ; oh, hurry,
fulfil your vows – the treasures of this world
are treacherous – learn this from your queen – no more now.
Farewell now, friends – farewell, farewell forever.

[*She turns away from them quickly. All leave, only* MELVILLE *remains*]

All temporal accounts are settled now.
I hope to leave this world as no man's debtor.

Only one thing remains which could prevent
my anxious soul from rising, free, serene.

Melville Reveal it to me. Ease your mind. Entrust
your troubles to a loyal friend.

Mary I stand
poised on the brink of all eternity,
soon to stand before the judge of all things,
but I have not yet made my peace with Him.
I am denied a priest of my own church,
and I refuse to accept the sacrament
from heretic ministers. I wish to die
in the true faith of Holy Mother Church,
my only hope and earnest of salvation.

Melville Make your mind easy. Heaven accepts the wish
in token of fulfilment. Tyrants chain
the hands; the heart's devotion rises free
to God. Faith breathes life into the dead word.

Mary Melville, the heart is insufficient. Faith
demands a guarantee on earth, to justify
its claim to Heaven's grace. It was for this
that God became a man, containing all
the invisible attributes of his divinity
within his visible body. And the church,
it is, both holy and sublime, that builds
the ladder by which we may mount to Heaven.
She is called the Universal Catholic Church:
only the faith of all can strengthen faith.
Where thousands worship and adore, the glow
bursts into flame, the soul mounts up to Heaven
on wings. Oh, they are happy who can gather
to pray together in the house of God!
The candles blaze, the altar gleams in gold,
the bell rings out, and incense fills the air,
the bishop stands in pure and splendid vestments,
he takes the chalice, blesses it, and proclaims
the miracle of Transubstantiation.
In the conviction of their faith, the people
sink to their knees before the Real Presence.
And I alone am exiled: in my prison
the grace of Heaven cannot penetrate.

Melville You cannot say that. It is with you now.
Believe in the omnipotence of God.
The barren staff flowers in the hand of faith.

He who struck water from the living rock
can raise an altar in this prison, change
the corporal nourishment within this cup
into the blood and body of Our Lord.
[*Takes the chalice standing on the table*]

Mary Do I understand you? Yes, I do.
Here is no priest, no church, no sacrament.
Yet our redeemer speaks to us and says;
Where even two are gathered in my name,
I am in the midst of them. What is it
that consecrates the priest to be God's mouthpiece?
His purity of heart, and blameless life.
You are a priest, then, although not ordained.
A messenger from God, to bring me peace.
I wish to make my last confession to you,
and receive absolution at your hands.

Melville If your heart longs so ardently for grace,
the Lord will work a miracle to comfort you.
You say here is no priest, no church, no host?
You are mistaken. All of them are here.
I am a priest: in order that I might
hear your last confession, make your peace
with God before you die, I have received
the seven holy orders and I bring
this host, from the Holy Father, blessed by him.
[*He bares his head, at the same time showing her a host on a golden patten*]

Mary Oh, must such heavenly joy be granted me
upon the very threshold of my death?
As an immortal, coming down upon
a golden cloud, as once the Apostle
was led by the angel from his prison bonds,
no bars, no keepers sword, no bolted door
restraining him in his triumphal march
until he blazed in glory in the cell,
so Heaven's messenger now surprises me
here, where all earthly saviours have failed me!
– And you, my servant once, are now the servant
of the Most High God: you are His Holy Word.
As you have knelt to me, in former times,
so I now lie now before you in the dust.
[*She goes on her knees before him*]

Melville [*Making the sign of the cross over her*]
In the name of the Father, Son, and Holy Ghost,
Mary of Scotland, have you searched your heart?
Do you swear and promise to confess
the truth before the God of truth?

Mary I swear it.
My heart lies open before you and Him.

Melville Daughter, what sins lie heavy on your conscience
since last you reconciled yourself with God?

Mary My heart was filled with hatred and with envy:
I have been eaten up with thoughts of vengeance.
I hoped my trespasses would be forgiven,
but could not pardon trespasses against me.

Melville Do you repent, and earnestly desire
to make your peace before you leave this world?

Mary As truly as I hope for God's forgiveness.

Melville What other sins do you accuse yourself of?

Mary It was not only by the sin of hate
that I offended Heaven, but still more
by that of carnal love. My heart was turned
in vanity towards a man who has
abandoned and betrayed me faithlessly.

Melville Do you repent, and has your heart abjured
this worldly idol and turned back to God?

Mary That was the hardest struggle I have had:
but now that final earthly bond is shed.

Melville What further sins lie heavy on your conscience?

Mary An early crime of blood, long since confessed,
harrows me with new fear, gives me no rest,.
I see it, now my last reckoning's to be made,
looming up darkly before Heaven's gate.
I caused the King, my husband, to be killed,
and gave my hand, and heart, to the seducer.
Though rigorous penances brought absolution, deep
inside my soul there is a worm that will not sleep.

Melville Your heart accuses you of nothing more?
No sin yet unconfessed, not yet absolved?

Mary Now you know all that lies upon my heart.

Melville Remember an all-knowing God can hear you.
Think of the penalties that Holy Church
exacts for false or incomplete confessions.
That is the sin against the Holy Ghost.

Mary May the Lord's mercy give me victory
in my last struggle, inasmuch as I
have hidden nothing knowingly from you.

Melville What? Would you hide from God the very crime
for which man's justice sends you to your death?
You have said nothing of the part you played
in aiding Babington's conspiracy?
Your earthly life is forfeit for that act.
Would you lose everlasting life because of it?

Mary I do not fear to face eternity:
before another hour has passed I shall
be standing in the presence of my judge,
but I repeat: I have finished my confession.

Melville Consider well; our judgments can deceive us.
Perhaps, by sly equivocation, you
avoid the word that makes you guilty, while
your will, your thoughts were party to the crime.
But no amount of mental juggling will
deceive the eye of flame that knows your hearts.

Mary Although I summoned all the Kings of Europe
to liberate me from this shameful bondage,
never in thought, or word, or deed, did I
aim at the life of my antagonist.

Melville The testimony of your secretaries
was false then?

Mary. It is just as I have told you.
Heaven will judge their depositions.

Melville You mount the scaffold, then, secure in innocence?

Mary This death which I have not deserved, God sends
to absolve me from my early crime of blood.

Melville [*Making the sign of the cross over her*]
Go then, make reparation by your death.
Blood will acquit you of a deed of blood.
It was your woman's frailty made you sin:
these earthly weaknesses do not pursue

the blessed soul to Heaven. I do here,
by virtue of the power vested in me
to bind and loose, absolve you of your sins.
As you believe, so may you find salvation.
Receive His body, which He gave for you.
[*He gives her the host*]
Receive His blood, which He has shed for you.
[*He takes the cup from the table, consecrates it with a silent prayer, and hands it to her. She hesitates, then declines it with a gesture*]
Do not hold back. The Holy Father grants you
this dispensation in the face of death,
to exercise the privilege of kings,
and priests.
[*She accepts the cup*]
Now as your earthly body has become
a part of God, so shall you be conjoined
eternally with Him in paradise,
where there shall be neither guilt, nor lamentation,
where you shall live to all eternity.

[*He puts the cup down. Hearing a noise outside, he covers his head, and goes to the door.* MARY *remains in prayer. He returns*]

There still remains one harsh ordeal for you.
Do you feel strong enough to conquer all
stirrings of bitterness and hate?

Mary There will
be no relapse. My hate and love I have
offered up to God.

Melville Then be prepared
to meet Lord Burleigh and the Earl of Leicester.
They are here.
[*Enter* BURLEIGH, LEICESTER, *and* PAULET. LEICESTER *remains standing at some distance, his eyes on the ground. Seeing his unease,* BURLEIGH *steps between him and the* QUEEN]

Burleigh I come, my Lady Stuart, to receive
your last commands.

Mary My Lord, I have to thank you.

Burleigh I am commanded by Her Majesty
to approve any reasonable request.

Mary My last requests are set down in my will.
Sir Amyas Paulet, I have given it

to you, and ask that it be faithfully
and duly carried out.

Paulet You have my word.

Mary I ask you further to allow my servants
to go unhindered and unharmed to France
or Scotland, or whatever place they please.

Burleigh It shall be as you wish.

Mary And since my body
is not to rest in consecrated ground,
I beg you, let my servant take my heart
and bring it to my family in France.
– Ah, it was always there!

Burleigh It shall be done.
Do you have any further –

Mary Bring the Queen
of England greetings from her sister – say
that I forgive her for my death with all
my heart, and ask forgiveness in my turn
from her, for my impetuosity
and violence yesterday. May God preserve her,
and grant she may yet reign many happy years.

Burleigh Will you not reconsider your refusal
to see the deacon of our church?

Mary My peace
with God is made. Sir Amyas Paulet,
I have, though through no willing fault of mine,
caused you great sorrow, robbed you of the staff
of your old age. – Oh, let me hope that you
will not remember me with hatred, sir –

Paulet [*Giving her his hand*]
God be with you, Lady, go in peace.

[KENNEDY *and the other women come in, with horrified expressions, followed by the* SHERIFF, *with a white staff. Armed men can be seen through the open door behind him*]

Mary What is it, Hannah? Ah, the time has come.
The Sheriff's here to take me to my death.
Now is the time to part. Farewell! farewell!
You, sir, and this my loyal waiting-woman
will both accompany me on my last walk.
I take it you, my Lord, have no objection.

Burleigh Nor do I have authority to grant it.

Mary So you, of course, deny me this small favour.
Respect my sex: who else is to attend me
at such a time? My sister cannot wish
our sex to be insulted in my person
by letting men lay their rude hands on me?

Burleigh We cannot allow a woman to ascend
the scaffold with you – all that weeping and wailing . . .

Mary She will not weep nor wail: I guarantee
my Hannah's strength of soul. my Lord, for charity,
do not divide me in my hour of death
from my devoted, lifelong nurse, and friend.
She bore me in her arms when I was born;
then let her gentle hand lead me to death.

Paulet [*To* BURLEIGH] Let it be so.

Burleigh So be it.

Mary Now there is
nothing for me on earth. My saviour!
[*She kisses the crucifix*]
As once your arms were stretched out on the cross,
open them now, Redeemer, to receive me.
[*Turning to go, her eye falls on* LEICESTER*, who had involuntarily turned to look at her as she went. Seeing him,* MARY *shivers, her knees refuse her, she is about to fall, when* LEICESTER *catches her in his arms. She looks at him earnestly for a few moments in silence. He cannot face her gaze. Finally she speaks*]
Lord Leicester, you have kept your word – you promised
your arm to lead me from this prison, and
now you see, I have it.
[*He stands crushed. She goes on*]
Nor, Leicester, was it freedom only that
I wished to owe to you. You were to make
my freedom dear to me. I wanted my
new life to be so happy in your love.
And now that I must bid this world farewell,
become a blessed spirit, far removed
from the temptations of an earthly love,
I can confess to you without a blush
this weakness which I conquered, Leicester.
Farewell, and if you can, fare happily.
You vied for the affections of two queens;

a tender loving heart, which you disdained,
betrayed, to win a proud one. Kneel to it.
May your reward not prove your punishment.
Farewell! – Now I have nothing left on earth.

[*She goes out, preceded by the* SHERIFF, *with* MELVILLE *and* KENNEDY *either side of her,* BURLEIGH *and* PAULET *following. The others gaze after her sorrowfully, until she disappears, then leave by the other door*]

Leicester And I am still alive. How shall I bear it?
Why will the roof not fall on me and crush me?
Is there no pit to open at my feet
and swallow the most wretched man alive?
What have I lost, what jewel thrown away?
She goes, transfigured, half a saint already;
my portion is the torments of the damned.
But where is the resolve with which I came
coldly to choke the promptings of my heart?
calmy to watch her head fall, while I stood apart?
And did her presence reawaken shame?
Must she entwine me closer in her death?
– To melt in womanly tears of tender pity,
no longer quite accords with my behaviour.
A happy love is hardly in my stars.
My face must be a rock, my heart encased
in steel. If you would profit from a crime,
you must pursue it, boldly, all the time.
Beware of pity: my eyes must be dry,
they must be witnesses, and watch her die.
[*Starts decisively to the door where* MARY *went, but stops halfway*]
It is no use: the horror masters me –
I cannot see her die – Ha! – what was that?
Beneath my feet: they are preparing for
their dreadful work. Now, I can hear voices –
I must leave this house where death and terror wait.
[*He goes to escape by another door, but finds it locked, and starts back*]
Is it a God that pins me to the floor?
And must I hear what I so dread to see?
That is the deacon now – exhorting her –
she interrupts him – now – she prays aloud –
her voice is firm – now silence – a great silence –
I can hear nothing but the sobs of woman –
they are taking off her veil – moving the footstool –
she kneels down on the cushion – puts her head –

[*After speaking the last words with rising terror, he is silent for a moment. Then he shudders convulsively and collapses in a faint, at the same time as a muffled uproar of voices sounds from below, continuing for a long time*]

Scene 2

[*The* QUEEN*'s Apartments*]

[ELIZABETH *enters by a side door, her walk and gestures expressing extreme uneasiness*]

Elizabeth Nobody here yet – and no news – will it
never be evening? Has the sun stopped still
on its way through Heaven? How much longer
must I be kept upon the rack? This waiting!
Has it been done? Or has it not? I dread
whichever it is, yet I dare not inquire.
Lord Leicester does not come, nor does Lord Burleigh,
whom I appointed to carry out the sentence.
If they have both left London, it is done:
the arrow is launched, flies, strikes, has struck already –
who's there?
[*Enter a* PAGE]
You are alone. Where are the Lords?

Page My lord of Leicester and the Lord High Treasurer –

Elizabeth [*In great suspense*]
Where are they?

Page Not in London.

Elizabeth No? Then where?

Page Nobody was able to inform me.
Just before daybreak, it would seem, both lords
left London secretly, and in great haste.

Elizabeth [*A triumphant outburst*]
Now I am Queen of England!
[*Paces in great excitement*]
You, there, go –
send for the – no, stay here. So. She is dead.
At last there's room for me upon this earth.
– Why do I shake? What is this fear that grips me?
My fear is buried in the grave; who dares to say

I did it? I shall show no lack of tears
for her. [*To the* PAGE] Tell Davison, the secretary,
to come immediately, and call the Earl
of Shrewsbury – but here he comes in person.
[*Exit* PAGE]
Talbot, welcome. What wind blows you here?
Surely no trifling matter, if it brings
you here at this late hour.

Shrewsbury Your Majesty,
my deep anxiety for your good name
prompted me to go to the tower today,
to visit Mary Stuart's secretaries,
who are imprisoned there. The governor
in some embarrassment refused to let
me see them, until I had threatened him.
Dear God, the sight of them! The Scotsman, Curle,
with matted hair and mad eyes, like a man
pursued by furies, lay on his bunk. The wretch
had barely recognised me when he threw
himself at my feet – screaming and clutching at
my knees, in desperation, like a worm
writhing before me, begging, imploring me
to tell him what had happened to his Queen.
Rumours that she had been condemned to death
had filtered through the thick walls of the Tower.
When I confirmed it was the truth, and added
it was his evidence that caused her death,
he sprang up in a frenzy, and attacked
his cell-mate, pulled him to the ground with all
a madman's strength, and tried to throttle him.
We were barely able to wrest the victim from
his frantic grasp. And then he turned his rage
upon himself, and beat his breast in frenzy,
cursing himself and his accomplice with
all the devils in Hell. He said he had
perjured himself – the letters to Babington
which he had said were genuine, were forged;
he had put down different words from what the Queen
dictated to him; the other secretary,
the villain Nau, had put him up to it.
Then he ran over to the window, and
flung it open with furious strength, and screamed
down to the street, till everyone came running,

he was the secretary of Mary Stuart,
he was the villain who accused her falsely,
he had borne false witness, and he was accursed.

Elizabeth You said yourself the man was mad. The ravings
of lunatics prove nothing.

Shrewsbury But the madness
itself proves all the more. Your Majesty,
I must implore you, do not be too hasty.
Order a fresh investigation now.

Elizabeth Of course I shall – since you implore me, Talbot,
and not because I think the peers were over-
hasty in this affair. But have no fear –
a fresh investigation of the case.
– How fortunate that there's still time! No shadow
of doubt shall stain the honour of our crown.
[*Enter* DAVISON]
The warrant, Davison; I gave it to you.
Where is it?

Davison [*Astonished*] Warrant, Madam?

Elizabeth Which I gave
into your charge, sir, yesterday . . .

Davison My charge?

Elizabeth The mob were pressing me to sign it: I
followed their will, and signed, under duress.
Then, in the hope of gaining time, I gave
the paper into your safe keeping, sir.
You know all that I said. Now give it me.

Shrewsbury Give it to her, the case is altered now.
A fresh investigation has been ordered.

Elizabeth You do not need to think. Where is the warrant?

Davison A fresh investigation? Oh, my God!
I am a dead man.

Elizabeth [*Interrupting quickly*]
I trust, sir, you have not –

Davison [*In despair*] I am lost. I do not have it any more.

Elizabeth What? What?

Shrewsbury Great Heavens!

Davison Since yesterday
Lord Burleigh has it.

Elizabeth Aaah! You villain.
So that is how you follow my instructions.
Did I not tell you, guard it with your life?

Davison Your Majesty, that was not your command.

Elizabeth Are you suggesting that I am a liar?
When did I tell you to give it to Lord Burleigh?

Davison Not in so many words, but I –

Elizabeth But you presumed,
you abject little wretch, to put your own
interpretation on my words. To read
your own bloodthirsty meaning into them.
If, sir, your arbitrary meddling
brings some disaster in its train, you shall
pay for it with your life. You see, my Lord,
how they misuse my name?

Shrewsbury I see. Oh, God in Heaven!

Elizabeth What is it now?

Shrewsbury If Davison presumed
to act at his own risk, without your knowledge,
he must be brought before the House of Lords,
to be arraigned there of lèse-majesté,
because he has exposed your name to all
the detestation of posterity.

[BURLEIGH *enters, and goes down on one knee to the* QUEEN]

Burleigh Long live my royal mistress: and may all
the enemies of England perish like
the Stuart.

[SHREWSBURY *covers his face.* DAVISON *wrings his hands in despair*]

Elizabeth Tell me, sir, did you receive
the warrant from my hands?

Burleigh Madam, I did not:
it was from Davison I had it.

Elizabeth Did he give
it to you in my name?

Burleigh No, he did not.

Elizabeth And yet you could not wait to know my mind,
before you put it into execution.
The sentence was well-merited: the world
will not be able to find fault with us:
nevertheless your duty does not lie
in the anticipation of our mercy.
You therefore shall be banished from our presence.
[*To* DAVISON]
For you, sir, a severer doom awaits:
you have exceeded your authority
outrageously, and wantonly betrayed
a sacred trust. Let him be taken to
the Tower at once: it is my will that he
be there arraigned upon a capital charge.
– Talbot! The only honest man that I have found
among my counsellors, from now on you
shall be my confidant, my guide, my friend.

Shrewsbury Do not send your truest friends to exile,
nor send to prison those who only acted
on your behalf, and, now, for you, keep silent.
And as for me, great Queen, permit me now
to render up again the Seal of England,
with which you trusted me these twelve long years.

Elizabeth [*Taken aback*] No, Talbot. You will not desert me now?

Shrewsbury Your pardon, Madam, I am far too old.
And this right hand has grown too stiff to set
its seal upon your latest acts.

Elizabeth I am
abandoned by the man who saved my life?

Shrewsbury I have done very little – I could not
preserve the better part of you. Long life
and happiness to your gracious Majesty!
Your rival's dead. You have from this day forward
no more to fear, and no more to respect.
[*Exit*]

Elizabeth [*To* KENT *who enters*]
Summon Lord Leicester here.

Kent His Lordship begs
to be excused. He has taken ship for France.

[ELIZABETH *masters herself, and stands, calm and composed. The curtain falls*]

Joan of Arc

Characters

Charles VII, *King of France*
Queen Isabeau, *his mother*
Agnès Sorel, *his mistress*
Philip the Good, *Duke of Burgundy*
Count Dunois, *the Bastard*
La Hire and Du Chatel, *royal officers*
Archbishop of Rheims
Chatillon, *a Burgundian knight*
Raoul, *a knight of Lorraine*
Talbot, *the English general*
Lionel and Fastolf, *English commanders*
Montgomery, *a Welshman*
Councillors, *from Orleans*
An English Herald
Thibaut d'Arc, *a rich sheep-farmer*
Margot, Louison and Joan, *his daughters*
Etienne, Claude-Marie and Raimond, *their suitors*
Bertrand, *another farmer*
The apparition of a Black Knight
Charcoal burner, his wife and son
Soldiers and people, royal servants, bishops, monks, marshals, magistrates, court personnel and other non-speaking characters in the coronation procession

Prologue

[*A country landscape. A saint's image in a shrine, and a tall oak tree.* THIBAUT D'ARC. *His three* DAUGHTERS. *Three young* SHEPHERDS, *their suitors*]

Thibaut Neighbours, and friends: yes, we are Frenchmen still,
free citizens and masters of the lands
our fathers ploughed before us, for today.
Who knows what masters we shall have tomorrow?
On every side the English banners float
victorious: their cavalry treads down
our crops: the gates of Paris have already
been opened to the conqueror, and the ancient
crown of St Denis has been placed upon
the head of a princeling of a foreign line.
The rightful heir of France must wander now,
an outcast refugee through his own kingdom.
Meanwhile his cousin and the premier peer
of France, the duke of Burgundy, has joined
the enemy, led by that bird of prey, his mother.
Villages and towns burn all around,
and all the while the smoke of ruin rolls
nearer and nearer to our peaceful valley.
Therefore, dear friends, with God's help, I'm resolved.
while I still can, to see my daughters married.
In times like these, women need our protection,
and true love helps to make our burdens lighter.

[*To the first* SHEPHERD]

Etienne, now, you've spoken for my Margot,
our fields adjoin: now let your hearts be joined –
a good foundation for a happy marriage.
Claude-Marie, you say nothing, and Louise
looks at the ground? Should I forbid the love
of two hearts that have found each other, simply
because you have no wealth to offer me?
Who has wealth nowadays, when farms and houses
lie at the mercy of the nearest foe – or fire?
The only stormproof shelter in these times
is a good man's love.

Louison Father!

Thibaut Louison!

Louison [*Embracing* JOAN] Sister!

Thibaut I give you thirty acres each, along
with outbuildings and livestock, and may God
be good to you, as He has been to me.

Margot [*Embracing* JOAN] Make Father happy. Follow our example,
and crown his happiness with a triple wedding.

Thibaut Go and get ready; the wedding is tomorrow,
and the whole village must be here to celebrate.

[*The two couples go off arm-in-arm*]

There are your sisters to be married, Joan.
To see them happy is a comfort to my age,
but you, my youngest, cause me pain and grief.

Raimond What are you thinking? Scolding her like that?

Thibaut Here is this excellent boy; not one in all
the village is to be compared with him.
For three years now his feelings have been plain,
no less sincere for being unexpressed.
But you rejected him, reserved and cold.
and no one else can win a smile from you.
I see you in the first full flush of youth:
this is your spring, this is your time of Hope,
your beauty is in flower, and still I wait
in vain for Love to flower and come to fruit.
I don't like it at all: it points to some
serious error in Nature when the heart
closes itself to feeling at your age.

Raimond That is enough now, let the girl alone.
Joan's love is like a delicate, tender fruit:
perfection must have time to grow to ripeness.
She still prefers to wander on the hillsides,
and leaves the open heath reluctantly
to come among people and their petty cares.
Sometimes, when I am in the valley, I
watch her, in silent wonder, on the uplands,
standing above her flock, so noble in
appearance, her gaze intently fixed upon
the little world below her, and she seems
to be in touch with higher things, almost
as if she came from some age not our own.

Thibaut That is precisely what I do not like!
She avoids the happy company of her sisters,
leaving her bed before first light to seek
the lonely hills: and in those hours of darkness
when folk are gladdest of each other's company,
she slips out, like some solitary owl,
into the dusk and gloom of the haunted night,
making her way up to the crossroads, where
she holds some secret conversation with the winds.
Why does she always choose that spot? why is
it there and only there she drives her flocks?
I've watched her sit and think for hours on end,
under the Druid's tree, which Christian souls
will not go near – the place is eerie, some
spirit of evil has lived beneath that tree
since heathen times – the old ones in the village
tell terrifying tales about the tree:
how you can often catch the sound of voices,
strange and uncanny, coming from its dark branches:
once I was passing it myself, at nightfall,
and saw this ghostly woman sitting there,
stretching a withered hand out of her cloak,
as if to say "Come here!": you may be sure
I quickened my step and offered up a prayer.

Raimond [*Pointing to the image in the shrine*]
It is the holy influence of the shrine
that brings your daughter here, and not the Devil.

Thibaut Oh, no! No! Not for nothing have I had
warnings in dreams and visions. Three times now
I've seen her, sitting on the royal throne
in Rheims Cathedral, on her head a crown
of seven stars, and in her hand a sceptre,
out of which three golden lilies sprouted,
while I, her father, and her sisters, and
princes, bishops, lords, the King himself
all knelt to her – how does such splendour come
to our poor house? It presages disaster.
The dream was sent to show me, and to warn me
about the idle vanity of her heart.
She is ashamed because she is low-born:
just because God has blessed her, outwardly
and inwardly, with faculties beyond
the other shepherd girls here in the valley,

she is puffed up with spiritual pride.
By that sin fell the angels: pride it is
gives Satan purchase on the souls of men.

Raimond Who is more modest, or more virtuous than
this child of yours? Has she not made herself
the willing servant of her elder sisters?
Her qualities would raise her far above
all others, yet you see her, like a maid,
performing the most menial tasks in quiet
humility. The livestock and the planting
thrive on her management: whatever she
sets her hand to is rewarded with
amazing, inexplicable good fortune.

Thibaut Yes, inexplicable. I feel a sort
of shudder at a blessing of this kind.
Enough – I'll say no more – I do not wish
to say another word. Should I accuse
my own dear child? All I can do is warn her,
and pray for her. Warn her, though, I must,
not to go near the tree, nor be alone,
not dig for roots, nor to prepare concoctions,
nor scratch out secret patterns in the sand.
The spirit world is easily aroused:
it lies in wait, under the thinnest cover,
for the slightest word to call it into life.
Do not be on your own, then: it was in
the wilderness that Satan tempted Christ.

[*Enter* BERTRAND, *carrying a helmet*]

Raimond Quiet! Bertrand, back from town. Look what
he's carrying.

Bertrand You look surprised to see
me with this strange contraption.

Thibaut Yes, we are.
How did you come by it, and why should you
bring this ill-omen to a land of peace?

[JOAN, *who up to now has taken no interest in the scene, gradually becomes attentive, and moves nearer in*]

Bertrand I hardly know myself how I came by it.
I was buying iron tools in Vaucouleurs:
there was a crowd of people in the market –

some refugees had brought bad news from Orleans –
the whole town seemed to have gathered in alarm,
and as I forced a passage through the crowd,
a dark-faced gypsy woman, carrying
this helmet, came right up to me, and stared
at me, and said "My son, you're looking for a helmet,
I know you're looking for one. There! Take this!
It's yours for next to nothing." And I said:
"Go to the soldiers; I don't need a helmet.
I'm just a farmer." But she wouldn't be
content with that, and went on "Who can dare
to say he does or doesn't need a helmet?
A steel roof for the head is nowadays
better than a stone one for the house."
She kept on, following me through the streets,
forcing the thing on me I didn't want.
I looked at it, saw it was fine and bright,
and fit to go on any great knight's head,
and as I weighed it doubtfully in my hand
wondering at the strangeness of it all,
the woman suddenly was gone, the stream
of people carried her away, and left
me standing with the helmet in my hands.

Joan [*Grasping for it eagerly*]
Give it to me!

Bertrand What would you want with it?
It's nothing for a girl.

Joan [*Snatching the helmet from him*]
The helmet's mine!

Thibaut What is the matter with the girl?

Raimond Just let
her have it. It will suit her well: she has
a man's heart in that body. Only think
how she fought off that wolf that caused such havoc
among our flocks, the terror of our shepherds;
how, on her own, the lion-hearted girl
fought with the beast and tore the lamb away
out of its very jaws. However brave
the one who wears this helmet, it could never
suit any more than her.

Thibaut [*To* BERTRAND] But tell us what
the news was which the refugees had brought.

Bertrand Pray Heaven help the king and spare the country!
We have been beaten in two heavy battles.
The enemy is in possession of
the whole of France up to the Loire, and now
he brings his whole force to besiege Orleans.

Thibaut Heaven protect the King!

Bertrand Artillery
is being brought in from all sides in countless
quantities, and like a swarm of bees
darkening the hive in summer, or a cloud
of locusts falling from the darkened sky
and covering the fields for miles around,
a swarm of soldiers poured into the plains
around Orleans: and in the camp is heard
a Babel of tongues, confused and deafening:
since the powerful Duke of Burgundy has brought
his vassals here as well, from Luxemburg
Liege and Hennegau, Namur, Brabant,
Ghent, Zeeland, Utrecht, Holland, and as far
North as West Friesland, to besiege Orleans.

Thibaut That is the saddest thing about this struggle,
that French arms should be used against France herself.

Bertrand And one can see the old queen-mother too,
the arrogant Isabella of Bavaria,
riding in full armour through the camp,
stirring the men up, with her poisonous speeches
against the King, her son.

Thibaut God's curse on her! And may He bring her down
as He did Jezebel.

Bertrand The siege is being led by the destroyer
of the Moors, the powerful Salisbury,
along with Lionel, a lion indeed,
and Talbot, who mows down our men in battle.
They have all sworn, in their overweening pride,
to give our women to their soldiers, and
to put our soldiers to the sword.
They have put up four observation towers
to overlook the town: and from above
the Earl of Salisbury looks down and counts
the people hurrying about the streets.
Thousands of tons of missiles have been hurled

into the town: the churches lie in ruins,
and the great tower of Notre Dame hangs down
its noble head. And they have undermined
the walls with powder magazines, so that the town
stands terror-stricken on a pit of Hell,
expecting every hour to fly in pieces

[JOAN *listens with intense attention, putting on the helmet*]

Thibaut Where were the swords of our brave leaders, then?
Saintrailles, La Hire, Dunois the Bastard, that
the enemy was able to push forward
so irresistibly? Where was the King?
Was he content to watch his country's ruin,
to see his cities all reduced to rubble?

Bertrand The court is at Chinon, but he lacks troops,
he cannot stay in the field: and what use is
the leader's courage or the hero's arms,
when panic paralyses all the army?
A terror, almost as if ordained by Heaven,
has seized upon the hearts even of the bravest.
The generals issue their commands in vain:
like sheep that huddle fearfully together
at the howling of the wolf, all Frenchmen now,
regardless of their former reputation
for valour, seek the safety of their castles.
One knight alone, or so I hear, has raised
a little band of soldiers for the King.

Joan [*Quickly*] What is his name?

Bertrand Baudricour. But he
will have no little difficulty outwitting
the enemy's intelligence, if he has
two English armies following at his heels.

Joan Where has he halted? Tell me, if you know.

Bertrand Not more than one day's march from Vaucouleurs.

Thibaut What's it to you, girl? Asking about things
that don't concern you.

Bertrand They in Vaucouleurs,
seeing the enemy so powerful, and no hope
of any more protection from the King,
have all resolved to go over to Burgundy.

That way we shall escape a foreign yoke,
staying with our own royal line: who knows
but that we may not serve the king again,
if he and Burgundy are reconciled.

Joan [*As if inspired*] No treaties! No surrender! The deliverer
is on the way, already armed for battle.
Before Orleans the enemy's luck will founder:
his cup is full, now it is harvest time.
The virgin with the sickle in her hand
will mow him down in his pride, and snatch his glory
back down from the stars where he had lodged it.
No weakening! No retreat! Before the crops
have turned to gold, before the moon is full,
no English horse shall water at the Loire.

Bertrand Oh, come, the age of miracles is over.

Joan No! It is not! A white dove will fly up,
brave as an eagle, to attack these vultures
that tear our land apart. She will bring down
the traitor Burgundy, Talbot, the hundred-handed,
the heaven-stormer, and that Salisbury,
profaner of the temple, and all those
swaggering islanders shall be driven before her
like lambs to slaughter: God will be at her side,
the God of battles, who will seek her out,
a trembling virgin, through whom he will show
his power on earth, for he is King of Kings.

Thibaut What has possessed the girl?

Raimond It is the helmet
gives her these warlike thoughts. Look at your daughter!
Her eyes are flashing and her cheeks are flushed.

Joan And shall this country fall? this country of
such fame, more beautiful than any that
the sun shines on; this paradise of lands,
which God loves as the apple of his eye:
is it to submit to foreign shackles?
In France the heathen power was forced to halt;
the ashes of St Louis rest in France;
from France they left to free the Holy Land.

Bertrand [*Astonished*] Listen to her! Where does she receive
this revelation from? You, her father:
God has given you a marvellous child.

Joan We shall not have our own kings any more:
the king who never dies shall vanish from
the earth: the king whose arm protects
the sacred plough, and shields the pasture lands,
makes the earth fertile, leads his subjects out
to Freedom, gathers his cities round his throne,
frightens the wicked and protects the weak,
who feels no envy, since he is the greatest,
who is both man and angel of compassion
upon this hostile earth. The throne which shines
with gold is a sure refuge for the outcast.
There, there is power and mercy to be found,
to confound the guilty, while the just draw near
in trust, to sport with lions at its feet.
How can the stranger king, come from abroad,
none of whose ancestors have found repose
within this land, how then can he love it?
He has not shared his youth with our young men,
our language sparks no feelings in his heart,
how can he be a father to his children?

Thibaut Now God protect the country and the king!
We are just peaceful countrymen, who have
no notion how to wield a sword, or curb
a war-horse: let us wait in patience,
to see whom victory will make our master.
God will decide the fortunes of this war:
our master is the one who is anointed
and crowned at Rheims. Come on now, back to work!
and mind our business. We can let the great
and powerful of the earth decide its fate.
Indifferent to destruction at the hand
of war, the earth remains: ours is the land.
Let flames devour our villages, and let
the warhorse trample down the ripening grain:
with a new spring new seed is born again:
houses can be rebuilt: men can forget.

[*All go out except* JOAN]

Joan Mountains, much-loved meadows, dear, quiet valleys,
Joan bids you all a long, a last farewell.
The fields I watered, and the trees I planted,
show fresh and green again. Farewell! the caves,
the cool springs, and the valley's voice, the echo
that would send back the songs I sang before;
farewell, you shall not see Joan any more.

Scenes of the joys of all my quiet days,
I leave you now behind, beyond, beneath.
Scatter yourselves, my lambs, and take your ways
to wander shepherdless upon your heath:
for I have now another flock to graze,
upon the field of danger, blood and death.
The spirit calls to me with tongues of fire,
what drives me is not earthly, vain desire.

He who in Sinai, on the mountain height,
appeared to Moses in the bush of flame,
and ordered him to stand in Pharoah's sight:
He who to the shepherd David came,
and chose the boy His champion in the fight,
who always favoured shepherds in His name;
He spoke out of the branches of the tree:
"Go forth! Bear witness in this world for Me.

With raw, rough iron your body shall be girt,
your woman's breast shall be encased in steel;
the love of Man may never move your heart,
Earth's sinful pleasures you shall never feel;
no marriage of which you shall be a part,
no child your woman's mission to fulfil.
But with war's honours I shall raise your name
above all women, to undying fame.

For when the last defeat of France seems near,
when in the battle even the bravest fail,
then will My standard become yours to bear,
and, like an eager thresher, with your flail
bring down the haughty conqueror in fear,
reverse his fortunes, over him prevail.
To France's hero-sons salvation bring,
free Rheims, and crown your true and lawful King!"

Heaven has vouchsafed to me a sign:
this helmet He has sent, it comes from Him.
His power in the metal is divine.
I flame with the courage of the Cherubim,
driving me on towards the battle line.
There, in the storm of steel, I sink, I swim:
I hear the war-cry, and turn to the foe:
the charger rears, and all the trumpets blow!

Act 1

[*The court of King Charles at Chinon*]

Dunois I cannot tolerate this any more.
I must renounce this king, who has forgotten
himself so shamefully. My heart bleeds in
my breast, and I could weep hot tears to see
our royal France quartered by the swords of thieves,
the noble cities, grown old with the kingdom,
giving their rusty keys up to the enemy,
while we waste valuable time here doing nothing.
I hear Orleans is beseiged, fly
from furthest Normandy, thinking to find
the king in arms and at his army's head:
instead I find him here, surrounded by
mountebanks, and minstrels, solving riddles,
and giving gallant parties for his mistress,
as if the land was wallowing in peace!
The Constable has left him, could not stand
the situation any longer: and
I too am resolved to abandon him,
and leave him to his wretched fate.

Du Chatel Here comes the King now!

Charles The Constable has sent me back his sword,
and given notice he will not serve
me any longer. In which case – dear God! –
all we are rid of is a troublesome man,
who sought to rule us quite without condition.

Dunois In such a time I would not be disposed
to greet the loss of <u>any</u> man so lightly.

Charles You say that just from love of contradiction:
you were no friend of his while he was here.

Dunois He was an arrogant, offensive fool
who never knew when to stop – but for this once,
he knows. He knows the time to leave a cause
is when there's no more honour to be gained.

Charles We're in one of our pleasant moods, I see:
I shan't disturb you. Du Chatel! there are
ambassadors from old King René, famous

singers; they must be entertained, and well.
See there's a golden chain for each of them.
And what is so amusing, pray?

Dunois To hear
how chains of gold fall from your lips like spittle.

Du Chatel Your Majesty! There is no money left
in the treasury.

Charles Then find some. Famous artists
shall never leave my court without reward.
It's they who make our sterile sceptre flower,
who weave the green, unfading leaves of life
into the barren circle of the crown.
Their mastery places them upon a level
with their masters: they set up the thrones
of their frail harmless kingdoms on their wish
alone, and are not circumscribed by space.
This higher world thus equally belongs
to those who rule men, and those who make their songs.

Du Chatel Your Majesty! as long as there were still
expedients, I tried to keep things from you:
now finally, necessity bids me speak.
You have no more to give away, – good grief! –
you have no more to live on from tomorrow!
The high tide of your fortune has retreated;
your treasury is at its lowest ebb.
The troops have not been paid yet, and are grumbling,
threatening to withdraw. I hardly know
what to advise to keep your royal household
provided with the bare necessities,
let alone in any fitting state.

Charles Mortgage the royal customs duties, and
get the Lombards to advance some money.

Du Chatel Sire! the customs duties are already
mortgaged for three years in advance.

Dunois Meanwhile
both lands and pledges go to rack and ruin.

Charles We still have several rich and fertile provinces.

Dunois As long as God and Talbot's armies spare them.
If Orleans is taken, you can go
and be a shepherd, like your friend King René.

Charles You never can resist a jibe at his
expense, but it was this king, who, although
dispossessed of all his lands, sent me
those rich gifts, even today.

Dunois Heaven forfend,
I hope he did not send the crown of Naples!
I hear it's going cheap, since he has taken
to playing shepherd.

Charles That is just a game,
a sort of joke he plays upon himself,
to make an innocent world of make-believe,
in a rough age of harsh realities.
But what he wishes, which is truly great,
is to reintroduce the good old times
when courtly love stirred men to deeds of courage,
and noble women sat in arbitration
on each nice point of etiquette. This is
the age in which the old man still lives happily,
seeking to recreate it here, like some
celestial city in the clouds, the way it is
described in the old songs. For this he has
set up a court of love, to which brave knights
can make their pilgrimage, where women are
enthroned in majesty and chastity,
where pure love once again can be the rule:
and he has picked me out as Prince of Love.

Dunois I am not yet so far degenerate
as to despise the paramount sway of Love,
seeing it is to him I owe my name,
my birth and everything that I inherit.
My father was the Prince of Orleans,
who never met the heart he could not win,
nor the enemy that could stand against him.
If you wish to deserve the title "Prince
of Love", then be the bravest of the brave.
My reading in those old books tells me that
love was always paired with chivalry,
and it was heroes sat at the round table,
not shepherds, if I am not misinformed.
The man who does not fight to defend Beauty
does not deserve to be rewarded by her.
This is the battlefield! Fight for your father's crown!
With your sword defend your property,

and the honour of all those noble ladies. Once
you have, through streams of enemy blood,
won back the crown of your ancestors, well, then
will be the time and suitable occasion
to crown yourself with myrtle.

Charles [*To a* COURTIER, *who enters*]
Yes, what is it?

Courtier Councillors from Orleans begging audience.

Charles Show them in.

[*Exit* COURTIER]

They will implore my help.
What can I do, who cannot help myself?

[*Enter three* COUNCILLORS]

Welcome, my loyal citizens of Orleans!
How are things with the city? Is she still
keeping the enemy off with her usual courage?

Councillor Alas, Your Majesty, the city is
in the direst straits, and every hour
the situation grows more desperate.
the outer walls are breached, the enemy
gains ground with each assault; the battlements
are undefended, for the men are all
thrown unremittingly against the enemy,
and few enough of them return. Meanwhile
the plague of hunger menaces the city.
Therefore Count Rochepierre, the town commander,
has, in this terrible emergency,
according to the rights of war, agreed
with the besiegers, to give up the city
on the twelfth day, if, within that time,
no force, sufficient to relieve the siege,
has signalled its appearance in the field.

[DUNOIS *makes a violent movement of anger*]

Charles So little time.

Councillor And so we come to you,
on a safe-conduct from the enemy,
to implore Your Majesty to pity us,
and send us help within the time allotted,
or else the city must surrender.

Dunois Could
Saintrailles have given his sanction to so vile
a treaty?

Councillor No, my lord. As long as he
was living, there would never have been talk
of peace or of surrender.

Dunois So he is dead?

Councillor He fell heroically on the city walls,
fighting for his king.

Charles Saintrailles is dead!
In that one man I lose an army.

[*A* KNIGHT *enters and speaks a few words in a low voice to* DUNOIS, *who exclaims in surprise*]

Dunois That as well!

Charles What now?

Dunois The Earl of Douglas sends to say
the Scottish troops have mutinied, and threaten
to withdraw if their arrears of pay are not
discharged immediately.

Charles Du Chatel!

Du Chatel [*Shrugging*] I cannot help Your Majesty.

Charles Pawn, promise,
all that we have, even to half our kingdom . . .

Du Chatel It will not help – there have already been
too many promises.

Charles The Scottish soldiers are the best I have!
They cannot leave me now, not now, they cannot!

Councillor [*Falling on his knees*]
Help us, Your Majesty! Think of our need!

Charles [*Despairingly*] Can I stamp armies from the ground? Will corn
grown in the palm of my hand? Tear me in pieces,
rip out my heart and turn it into coin.
Blood I can give you, but not men nor money.

[*He sees* SOREL *coming in, and hurries to her with arms outstretched.*]

Agnès! My love, my life! You come in time
to save me from despair. While I can still
fly to your arms, all is not lost, since you
are mine still.

Sorel [*Entering, carrying a casket*]
Oh, my dear Lord!

[*She looks round anxiously*]

Du Chatel? Dunois?
Is this true, then?

Du Chatel I fear so.

Sorel Is the need
really so urgent? Will the troops withdraw
for want of pay?

Du Chatel I am afraid so.

Sorel [*Pressing the casket on him*]
Here!
Here is gold! Here are my jewels! Melt
my silver down! Sell, mortgage all my castles!
Arrange a loan on my Provence estates!
Turn everything to money, see the armies
are satisfied. Go now and lose no time.

[*Pushing him out*]

Charles Well, Dunois? Du Chatel? Am I still poor,
while I possess this jewel among women?
Nobly born as I am – even the blood
of Valois is no better – she would be
an ornament to any throne in the world.
But she despises them, and wishes only
to be my love, and to be seen to be it.
Has she ever accepted from my hand
a present more expensive than a flower
in wintertime, or some exotic fruit?
She will accept no sacrifice from me,
and yet she sacrifices all for me,
wagering all her property and fortune
to prop the fortunes of my tottering house.

Dunois She is as mad as you are, throwing all
she has into a burning house, and trying
to put the fire out with a leaky bucket.

She will not save you, she will merely bring
herself to ruin with you –

Sorel Don't believe him!
He has risked his life a dozen times for you,
and now he's angry because I risk my money.
Have I not already given you
and freely, all I have of much more value
than gold or jewels, and am I now supposed
to keep my wretched fortune to myself?
Let us get rid of all superfluous
luxuries, let me set you an example
of renunciation. Turn your courtiers
into an army, turn your gold into steel,
decide now to throw everything you have
away, to win your crown back. Come with me!
Come! We shall share all dangers and privations;
we'll ride together, we'll expose our bodies
to the burning arrows of the sun; the clouds
will be our canopy, and the stones our pillows.
The roughest soldier will stop grumbling, when
he sees his king, no better than the meanest,
enduring and surmounting want and toil.

Charles [*Smiling*] A prophecy begins to be fulfilled,
a nun at Clermont made to me; she said
a woman would make me victor over all
my enemies, and win back my fathers' crown.
I looked for her among the enemy camp,
thinking to make peace with my mother. But
here is the heroine who will lead me on
to Rheims, and in whose love I shall find victory!

Sorel You will find it in the swords of your brave friends.

Charles I have great hopes of discord in their camp;
I have intelligence that all is not
just as it was between the Lords of England,
and cousin Burgundy. I therefore sent
La Hire to take a message to the Duke,
to see if we can bring our furious kinsman
back to the path of loyalty and duty.
I expect him back at any moment.

Du Chatel [*At the window*]
He
has just dismounted in the courtyard.

Charles Now,
this welcome messenger will let us know
whether it's victory or retreat. La Hire!

[*Going to meet* LA HIRE *as he enters*]

Do you bring us hope or not? Be brief.
What are we to expect?

La Hire Nothing, but what
your sword can get from him.

Charles So he will not
be reconciled. How did he take my message?

La Hire First, and before he even gives an ear
to your proposals, he demands that you
deliver Du Chatel to him, the man he calls
his father's murderer.

Charles And what if we
refuse this unacceptable condition?

La Hire The treaty may be looked on as still-born.

Charles And did you, as I asked you, challenge him
to fight with me in single combat, at
the bridge at Montereau, where his father died?

La Hire I threw your gauntlet down, and let him know
you would lay by your dignity, and fight
for your kingdom as a simple knight. He answered
that he could see no need to fight for what
he had already, but that if you were
so eager for a fight, then you would find him
at Orleans, where he means to go tomorrow:
and then he laughed, and turned his back on me.

Charles And was there no voice raised in Parliament
on the side of justice?

La Hire No. That voice was drowned
in party rage. Parliament has decreed,
you and your house have forfeited the crown.

Dunois The arrogance of slaves who would be masters!

Charles Did you make no approaches to my mother?

La Hire Your mother!

Charles Yes. How did she view the business?

La Hire [*After a moment of consideration*]
When I arrived at St Denis, it was
the day of the coronation, and all Paris
was decked out, as if for a victory.
In every street there were triumphal arches,
through which the King of England passed in state.
The road was strewn with flowers, and the mob
crowded around the carriage, yelling and shouting,
as if France had just won her finest victory.

Sorel Shouting and yelling as they tread upon
the heart of their own true and loving king.

La Hire I saw the boy, young Harry of Lancaster,
on the throne of St Louis, with both his proud uncles,
Bedford and Gloucester,standing at his side,
while the Duke of Burgundy went on his knees
before the throne to swear his land's allegiance.

Charles Oh my unworthy cousin! False, disloyal!

La Hire The boy was scared, and stumbled as he climbed
the steps up to the throne. The people muttered
something about ill omens, and a laugh
rang out among the crowd, and, at that moment,
your mother, the old queen, stepped forward, and . . .
I am appalled to speak of it . . .

Charles What happened?

La Hire She picked the boy up in her arms, and set him
up on your fathers' throne.

Charles Oh, mother, mother!

La Hire Even the Burgundian troops, inured
by now to blood and fury blushed to see it.
She guessed what they were thinking, and she turned
to face the crowd, and raised her voice to say:
"Frenchmen, you have me to thank for this.
I have cut down the old, sick trunk and planted
the healthy sapling, and have saved you from
the misbegotten son of an idiot father."

[*The* KING *covers his face.* SOREL *runs to him and folds him in her arms. All present express their disgust and horror*]

Dunois Wolf bitch! Bloodthirsty, rabid monster!

Charles [*After a pause, to the* COUNCILLORS]
Well, you have heard how matters stand with us.
Go back to Orleans, waste no more time here,
and tell my loyal city: I release her
from any oath of fealty sworn to me.
Let her seek mercy from the Duke of Burgundy:

Dunois What is this, Sire? Will you give up Orleans?

Councillor My royal master! Do not take away
your hand from us. Oh, do not give your loyal
city up to the tyranny of England!
She is the brightest jewel in your crown,
and none has been more faithful to your fathers.

Dunois Have we been beaten, then? Is it allowed
to quit the field before one blow is struck
to save the city? Is that how you think
to give away, with one lightly spoken word,
the finest city from the heart of France?

Charles Enough blood has been shed, and pointlessly!
The heavy hand of Heaven is against me.
My armies are defeated in every battle:
my parliament disowns me: in my capital
my people greet my enemy with frenzy:
my next of kin abandon and betray me:
and even my own mother suckles the brood
of hostile foreigners at the breast. Therefore
we shall draw back to the South bank of the Loire,
and submit ourselves to the all-powerful hand
of Heaven, which fights upon the English side.

Sorel Heaven forfend that we, despairing of
our cause, should turn our backs upon our country.
Your brave heart just cannot have framed those words.
My king's heroic spirit has been broken
by the vile acts of his unnatural mother.
You will soon be yourself again, and able
to counter bravely all the blows that Fate
is dealing you.

Charles [*Gloomily*] But might it not be true?
A dark and terrible curse is on the house
of Valois. God has cast us out. My mother's
depravity has brought the Furies down
upon our house. For twenty years my father

was mad, three elder brothers died before me.
It is the will of Heaven that the house
of Valois perishes with Charles the Sixth.

Sorel It will rise again in you! Have confidence
in yourself. Oh, it is not in vain that Heaven
was kinder to you than to all your brothers,
placing you, although the youngest son,
upon a throne you never could have looked for.
Your gentle nature is the medecine
for all the wounds that party rage inflicts
on France. You will put out the angry fires
of civil war – my heart tells me you will –
restore peace and our ancient monarchy.

Charles Not I. These rough and storm-tossed times demand
a stronger steersman at the helm. I might
have made a peaceful nation happy, but
not this desperate and savage people.
I cannot force my way through with my sword
into those hearts that hate has closed against me.

Sorel The people are dazzled, stunned: a sort of madness
possesses them, but that will pass. The day
is not far off when their old love for their
ancestral king, the love that's planted deep
in every Frenchman's heart, will reawaken,
and jealousy along with it, and the ancient
aversion that exists between two nations.
The victor will be destroyed by his own good fortune.
That is why you must not be too hasty
to quit the field, but fight for every inch
of ground, defend Orleans, as if your life
depended on it. Rather let all the ferries
be sunk and all the bridges burnt that carry you
over your kingdom's border, across the Loire
as if across the Styx.

Charles What I could do,
I have already done. I offered myself
in single combat for the crown. I was refused.
My people's blood is being spilt in vain:
my cities are collapsing into dust.
Should I be like the unnatural mother, who
let her own child be cut in two? Oh, no!
I shall renounce my child, so it may live.

Dunois What, Sire? Is that the language of a king?
Is that the way one gives away a crown?
The meanest of your subjects stakes his life
and all he has on what he loves and hates.
Let once the bloody sign of civil war
be hung out, and all men are partisans.
The ploughman leaves the plough, the housewife leaves
her distaff, children and old men take arms,
the townsfolk fire their cities, and the peasant
sets fire to his crops, to do you harm
or good, whichever will express his will.
He gives no quarter, and expects none, when
he fights for his honour, for his gods, or idols.
Stop this show of self-pity, then, which ill
becomes a king, and let war take its course
and burn its fury out. It was not you
who set it recklessly alight. The people
must sacrifice itself for King and Country.
that is the law and fate of nations, and
there is no Frenchman who would have it otherwise.
The nation is not worthy of the name,
that will not risk its all to save its honour.

Charles [*To the* COUNCILLORS]
Expect no more from me. I can do nothing.
God protect you.

Dunois May the god of battles
from now on turn his back on you, as you
have turned your back on your ancestral kingdom.
I shall desert you, since you desert yourself.
Not all the might of Burgundy and England,
but your own cowardice costs you your throne.
The kings of France were heroes once, but you
have had unsoldierly breeding, it would seem.

[*To the* COUNCILLORS]

The King has given you up, but I shall throw
myself into the fight for Orleans,
my native city, and perish in its ruins.

[*He starts to leave.* SOREL *detains him*]

Sorel No! Do not let him leave you in this anger.
His words are harsh, but his heart is true as gold.
This is the man who loves you, who has shed

his blood for you before. Dunois, confess,
the heat of the moment made you go too far.
And you, forgive him what was said in haste.
Oh, come, the pair of you. Let me reconcile
your hearts, before this disagreement bursts
into unquenchable, destructive flame.

[DUNOIS *stares fixedly at the* KING, *waiting for an answer*]

Charles [*To* DU CHATEL] We cross the Loire. See my equipment packed.

Dunois [*Quickly, to* SOREL] Goodbye.

[*He turns quickly and goes out, the* COUNCILLORS *following him*]

Sorel Oh, if he leaves us, we are truly lost.
La Hire, go after him – try to bring him round.

[LA HIRE *goes out*]

Charles Well, is the crown the only thing in the world?
Is it such pain and grief to part with it?
I'll tell you something that is harder still
to bear, and that is being imposed upon
by obstinate and domineering bullies,
being dependent on the favour of
a lot of arrogant, self-opinionated
vassals. That is the really hard thing for
a noble heart to bear, and bitterer far
than yielding to one's fate.

[*To* DU CHATEL]

Obey your orders!

Du Chatel [*Throwing himself at the* KING*'s feet*]
Your Majesty!

Charles I have decided. Not another word!

Du Chatel Conclude peace with the Duke of Burgundy.
There is no other way to save yourself.

Charles Is that what you advise? And is it your blood
that will be used to sign this treaty with?

Du Chatel Here is my head. I have risked it often enough
in battle for you. Now I willingly
place it upon the block for you. Appease
the Duke. Deliver me to everything
his rage can do to me, and let my blood
put out the fires of this ancient hatred.

Charles [*Looks at him for a moment, moved and silent*]
Is it true then? Are things as bad as that?
My friends, who see into my heart, propose
I tread the path of shame to my deliverance?
Yes, now I see how low I must have fallen,
if no one any longer trusts my honour.

Du Chatel Just think –

Charles Say nothing! Do not make me angry.
If I had to abandon twenty thrones,
I would not save myself at the expense
of a friend's life. Now do as you were ordered.
See my necessaries are embarked.

Du Chatel At once.

[*He rises and leaves.* SOREL *bursts into violent sobbing*]

Charles [*Taking her hand*]
Agnès, do not be sad. Beyond the Loire
there is another France, and we are travelling
towards a happier land. A milder sky
unmarred by any cloud smiles on us there,
the winds blow softer, and we are received
with gentler customs: it is the land of song,
and life and love may flower more freely there.

Sorel That I should ever have lived to see this day!
The king in banishment, the son compelled
to leave his fathers' house, to turn his back
upon the cradle of his childhood.Oh,
my dear, dear country! Now we have to leave you,
and we shall never again return in joy.

[LA HIRE *returns*]

You are alone. You have not brought him back?

[*Looking at him more closely*]

La Hire, what is it? What is that look supposed
to mean? Is there some new catastrophe?

La Hire Catastrophe has spent itself: the sun
shines out once more.

Sorel What do you mean?

La Hire [*To the* KING]
Call back
the councillors from Orleans.

Charles Why, what has happened?

La Hire Call them back. Your fortune's tide has turned.
A battle has been fought – you are victorious!

Sorel Victorious! The music of that word!

Charles La Hire! you are deceived with groundless rumours.
Victorious! I've no more faith in victories.

La Hire You will soon believe in greater miracles.
Here is the Archbishop, bringing the Bastard
back to your arms . . .

Sorel The fairest flower of victory
is to bring peace and reconciliation.

[*Enter the* ARCHBISHOP *of Rheims,* DUNOIS, DU CHATEL *and a knight in armour,* RAOUL]

Archbishop [*Leading the* BASTARD *to the* KING, *and joining their hands*]
Princes, embrace! Let bitterness and discord
vanish, since Heaven declares itself for us.

[DUNOIS *embraces the* KING]

Charles Put me out of doubt and of amazement.
What does this solemn seriousness portend?
What has brought about this sudden change?

Archbishop [*Bringing the* KNIGHT *forward to the* KING]
Speak!

Raoul We had brought sixteen companies to the field,
men of Lorraine, to reinforce your armies,
under the leadership of Baudricourt,
from Vaucouleurs. When we had reached the heights
by Vermanton, and gone down to the valley
of the Yonne, there stood the enemy upon
the plain in front of us, and when we looked
behind us, weapons glittered there as well.
We saw ourselves surrounded on all sides.
There was no hope of victory or flight.
The bravest hearts were dashed, and, in despair,
each man began to lay aside his weapons.
And while the generals discussed among
themselves what or what not to do, and still
unable to decide – before our eyes,
a miracle ! Suddenly, a girl stepped out

of the depths of the woods, a helmet on her head
like some goddess of war, and beautiful
yet at the same time terrifying. Her hair
fell in dark curls around her neck; a sort
of heavenly aura seemed to play about
her figure, as she raised her voice, to say:
"What are you afraid of, Frenchmen? Up,
attack the enemy: even if he should have
more soldiers than there are sands in the sea,
God and the Blessed Virgin lead you on!"
And then she seized the flag out of the hand
of the standard-bearer,and with dignity
and irresistible audacity,
strode to the head of the column. We, struck dumb
with wonder, almost as if against our wills,
followed the flag and her who carried it,
and made an onslaught on the enemy,
who, utterly amazed, stood motionless,
staring at the miracle taking place
before their very eyes – but suddenly,
as if the fear of God was in them, they
threw their weapons down, and turned and fled.
The entire army scattered across the field;
commands were useless, and the officers rallied
the men in vain: without a backward glance
the panic-stricken men and horses plunged
into the river-bed, and let themselves
be slaughtered without the least show of resistance.
It was no battle – it was butchery!
Two thousand enemy dead lie on the field,
not counting those the river swallowed up:
on our side, not a single man was lost.

Charles My God, that's strange! Miraculous and strange!

Sorel You say a young girl worked this miracle?
Where is she from? Who is she?

Raoul Who she is
she will reveal to no one but the King.
She calls herself a prophetess, sent by Heaven,
and promises to save Orleans before
the moon has changed. The men believe in her;
they're spoiling for a battle. She herself
follows the army and will soon be here.

[*Bells are heard, and the clashing of weapons*]

You hear that noise? The people welcome her.

Charles [*To* DU CHATEL]
Have her brought in.

[*To the* ARCHBISHOP]

What should one make of this?
A young girl brings me victory, and at
the very moment only God could help me?
That's hardly in the normal course of Nature:
might one not – Archbishop – trust in miracles?

Many Voices [*Offstage*] The maid! The maid! Hail the deliverer!

Charles She's here!

[*To* DUNOIS]

Sit in my place, Dunois, we'll see
just how miraculous this young girl is.
If she is inspired and sent by God,
she will know how to tell which is the King.

[DUNOIS *sits with the* KING *on his right, and* SOREL *next to him, the* ARCHBISHOP *and the rest opposite him, so that the area in the middle of the stage is clear.* JOAN *enters, accompanied by the* COUNCILLORS *and a number of* KNIGHTS, *who fill the rear of the stage: she steps forward, with dignity, and scrutinises the assembly one by one*]

Dunois [*After a deep and solemn silence*]
Are you the miracle-worker, then, the girl who all . . .

Joan [*Interrupting him, looking at him clear-eyed and with dignity*]
Bastard of Orleans! Would you tempt your God?
Get off that chair; it is no place for you.
My heavenly mission is to one far greater.

[*She walks resolutely up to the* KING, *goes on one knee before him, getting up again at once. All present express their astonishment.* DUNOIS *leaves his seat, and a space is left empty in front of the* KING]

Charles You see my face today for the first time.
Where does this knowledge come from?

Joan I saw you,
when no one else saw you, apart from God.

[*She approaches the* KING *and speaks confidentially*]

Only think back to this last night that's passed.
When all around lay buried in deep sleep,
you got up from your bed, and prayed to God.
Send all these here away, and I will tell you
the content of that prayer.

Charles What I confide
to Heaven, need not be concealed from men.
So tell me the content of my prayer, and I
shall doubt no longer you are sent by Heaven.

Joan You made three prayers: now, Dauphin, see if I
can tell you what they were. First, you implored
Heaven, if any ill-gotten wealth still clung
to the crown, or any other grievous sin,
not yet atoned for, dating from the days
of your forefathers, was responsible
for stirring up this tragic war, then Heaven
should take you as a sacrifice for your people,
and pour the vials of its wrath out on your head
alone.

Charles [*Recoiling in fear*]
Who are you, prodigy? Where are you from?

[*All express astonishment*]

Joan You then addressed a second prayer to Heaven:
that if it was God's will to take away
the sceptre from your house, and everything
your fathers, kings before you in this country,
possessed, you wished to keep three things:
peace of mind, friendship, and Agnès's love.

[*The* KING *hides his face, shaken with sobs; a movement of astonishment among all present. A pause*]

Shall I tell you what your third prayer was?

Charles No! Enough! I believe in you! No mortal
could know as much. You are inspired by God.

Archbishop Who are you, holy and miraculous girl?
What blessed country bore you? Speak! Who are
your parents, whom God has favoured so?

Joan My reverend Lord, my name is Joan: I am merely
the humble daughter of a sheep-farmer,
from the kings's village of Domremy, which lies
in the bishopric of Toul, and there I've kept

my father's sheep-flocks, since I was a child.
I often heard about the islanders
who'd come across the sea to make us slaves
and force us to accept a foreign king,
who did not love our people, and of how
they had already captured the great city
of Paris and had conquered all the country.
I used to pray, in tears, to the Blessed Virgin,
to save us from the shame of foreign chains,
and to preserve our true-born king from harm.
Outside the village where I was born there stands
a statue of the Virgin, very old,
where people often come in pilgrimage,
and nearby stands an oak-tree, which is famous
for working miracles: I used to love
to sit in its shadow while I watched the flocks.
And if a lamb got lost upon the hillsides,
a dream would always tell me where it was,
if I slept in the shadow of the oak.
And once, when I had sat a long night through,
under the tree, thinking and praying hard,
and keeping sleep at bay, the Holy Mother
appeared in front of me, carrying a sword
and a flag, but dressed in every other way
like a shepherdess, like me, and she spoke to me:
"Yes, it is me. Rise up, Joan. Leave the flocks.
The Lord has called you to another business.
Take this flag! Put on the sword! With them
go to destroy the enemies of my people!
And lead your King's son on to Rheims, and crown
him with the royal crown!" But I replied:
"How can I bring myself to do such things?
I'm just a girl, I don't know how to fight."
Then she went on: "A virgin without stain,
can accomplish all the good deeds in the world,
if she withstands the love that's <u>of</u> the world.
Only look at me. I was, like you,
a chaste maid, yet I gave birth to the Lord,
the Lord divine; I am myself divine!"
And then she touched my eyelids, and when I
looked up, the heavens were full of angels,
boys, holding white lilies in their hands,
and there was lovely music in the air.
And so, three nights on end, the Holy One

appeared to me, and called me: "Rise up, Joan!
The Lord has called you to another business."
The third night, when she came, then she was angry,
and spoke severely: "Woman's duty here
on earth is to obey, and patiently
to endure her heavy fate, and purify
herself with constant, unremitting service.
She who has served on earth is great in Heaven."
And as she spoke, the shepherdess's dress
fell from her, and she stood there, Queen of Heaven,
clad in the brightness of a thousand suns;
then golden clouds lifted her up, slowly
taking her from my sight, to Paradise.

[*Everyone is deeply moved. Agnès* SOREL, *in tears, hides her face on the* KING*'s breast*]

Archbishop [*After a long pause*]
Such heavenly proofs must silence every doubt
that worldly subtlety can cast on them.
Her actions plainly show she speaks the truth,
since God alone can work such miracles.

Dunois I trust her look more than her miracles,
the total innocence of her expression.

Charles And am I, wretched sinner, worthy of
such grace? That eye, unerring and all-seeing,
looks into me and knows my heart is humbled.

Joan Humility in great men lights the sky:
you lower yourself, God raises you on high.

Charles And are you saying I shall win this war?

Joan I will bring France in tribute to you, Sire.

Charles Orleans is not menaced any more?

Joan Sooner expect the Loire to catch on fire.

Charles I'll enter Rheims a conqueror, you say?

Joan Though twenty thousand foes should bar the way.

[*All the* KNIGHTS *present set up a din with their shields and lances, and show signs of enthusiasm*]

Dunois Give us the girl to march before us at
the army's head, and we will follow blindly,
wherever she leads us. Her prophetic eye
directs us, and this stout sword shall protect her!

La Hire We shall not fear the world in arms against us,
if she is at the head of our battallions.
The God of Victory walks by her side,
and in the battle she shall be our guide.

[*The* KNIGHTS *set up a terrific clatter of weapons and step forward*]

Charles Yes, holy virgin, you shall lead my army:
its leaders shall obey you. And this sword,
the emblem of supreme authority,
which the High Constable of France sent back
in anger, has now found a worthier hand.
Take it, holy prophetess, and henceforward . . .

Joan No! Not so, noble Dauphin!
Not through this instrument of earthly power
shall my Lord gain the victory. I know
another weapon by which I shall win.
Let me describe it as the vision taught me,
then send to have it brought here.

Charles Go on, Joan.

Joan Send to the ancient town of Fierbois,
there, in Saint Catherine's churchyard, is a vault,
where many old iron weapons lie in heaps,
the spoils of victories of long ago;
among them is the sword that I must fight with.
It has three golden lilies stamped along
its blade: that way it will be recognised.
Have the sword fetched; it is the one will bring you victory.

Charles Send somebody to do as she commands.

Joan And let me carry a white banner, with
a purple border, and the Queen of Heaven
and the beautiful Infant Jesus painted on it,
hovering above the world, for that is how
the Holy Mother showed me in the vision.

Charles It shall be done, just as you say.

Joan [*To the* ARCHBISHOP]
My Lord,
lay your priestly hand on my head, and speak
a blessing on your daughter.

[*She kneels*]

Archbishop You have come
to impart a blessing, rather than receive one.
"Go in the strength of God". We are unworthy sinners.

[JOAN *rises*]

Courtier A herald from the English general.

Joan Let him come in, for God has sent him here.

[CHARLES *signs to the* COURTIER, *who goes out. Enter the* HERALD]

Charles State your commission, Herald.

Herald Who is spokesman
for Charles of Valois, Count of Ponthieu?

Dunois Herald, you are insubordinate.
Disrespectful boy, have you the gall
to deny his title to the King of France
on his own soil? As an ambassador
you are protected, otherwise –

Herald France recognises one king only, and
that king lives in the English camp.

Charles Be silent, cousin! Your commission, Herald!

Herald The noble Lord of Salisbury, aggrieved
by all the blood that has been shed, and by
all that shall be shed in the future, is
holding back his soldiers, with their swords
still in their scabbards. Now, before Orleans
is taken by storm, he offers generous terms
of compromise.

Charles What are they?

Joan [*Stepping forward*]
Sire, allow
me to reply to him in place of you.

Charles Do so: decide if it will be peace or war.

Joan [*To the* HERALD]
Who sent you here, and who speaks here through you?

Herald The English general, the Earl of Salisbury.

Joan That is a lie! He does not speak through you:
only the living speak, and not the dead.

Herald The general is in the best of health,
and will survive to annihilate you all.

Joan He was alive when you last saw him, but
a shot from Orleans laid him low this morning,
as he was watching from the observation tower –
you laugh, because I tell you things that happened
so far away? If you do not believe
my words, trust your own eyes. You will overtake
his funeral upon your homeward journey.
Now, Herald, say your piece, what is your errand?

Herald Since you can tell things which cannot be known,
you will know what it is before I tell you.

Joan I do not need to know your message, but
you need to know mine, and to take my words
back to those generals who sent you here.
– King of England, and you, the Dukes of Bedford,
and Gloucester, acting as his viceroys,
make your account to the great King of Heaven
for all the blood that has been shed by you.
Surrender all the keys of all the cities,
which you have taken in defiance of
the will of Heaven, whose King now sends a virgin
to offer you peace or bloody war. So choose!
I tell you now, in order that you know:
the Son of Mary has not destined France
to be yours: rather Charles, my Lord and Dauphin,
to whom God has assigned the kingdom, shall
enter in royal triumph into Paris,
attended by the French nobility.
– Now, Herald, make all speed away from here:
before you're back in camp to report these scenes,
I, Joan the Maid, will be already there,
planting the flag of victory in Orleans.

[*She goes out, leaving a scene of turmoil*]

Act 2

Scene 1

[*A region enclosed by cliffs*]

[TALBOT *and* LIONEL, *the English commanders. Philip, Duke of* BURGUNDY. *The knights* FASTOLF *and* CHATILLON, *with soldiers and standards*]

Talbot Beneath these cliffs here let us make a halt,
and pitch a proper camp, and see if we
can rally our straggling forces once again,
who fled and scattered at the first alarm.
Man the heights there, and post reliable guards.
The night protects us from pursuit: unless
the enemy has wings as well, I have
no fear of his attacking. Nonetheless
we need to use the utmost caution, since
the enemy is bold, and we've been beaten once.

[*Exeunt* FASTOLF *with his men*]

Lionel Beaten! General, do not use that word
again. I cannot allow myself to think
how Frenchmen saw the backs of English soldiers
today. Orleans! Orleans! Grave of our renown!
England's honour lies slain upon your fields.
Disgraceful and ridiculous defeat!
Who will believe it in the years to come?
The victors of Crecy, Poitiers, Agincourt,
driven off the field, and by a woman!

Burgundy It must be some small comfort to us that
we were not beaten by men, but by the devil.

Talbot The devil of our own stupidity!
What, Burgundy, are princes frightened too
by the same ghosts that terrify the mob?
Your superstition is a poor disguise
for cowardice; your troops were first to fly.

Burgundy No one stood fast. It was a general rout.

Talbot No, Sir, it was on your wing it began.
You all came bursting into our camp, shouting:

"All hell has broken loose – the Devil fights
for France!", and that brought our men to confusion.

Lionel You can't deny, your wing was first to break.

Burgundy Only because the first attack was there.

Talbot The girl knew just where we were weakest, and
she knew just where to look to find the cowards.

Burgundy So I am to be blamed for this disaster?

Lionel If we'd been on our own, the English army,
– by God! – we never would have lost Orleans!

Burgundy Indeed you would not. In that case, you would
never have seen Orleans in the first place.
Who paved the way for you into this country?
held out the hand of friendship to you, when
you set foot on this foreign, hostile coast?
Who crowned your Henry king in Paris? Who
won the hearts of Frenchmen to his side?
By God! Without this strong right arm to lead you,
you wouldn't have seen the smoke from a French chimney.

Lionel If great words were great deeds, Duke, you would have
subdued the whole of France all by yourself.

Burgundy You're sulking now, because you lost Orleans,
and have to work your spleen off on your ally.
Why did we lose Orleans? Because of your greed.
The city was prepared to yield to me;
your envy and nothing else prevented it.

Talbot We were not laying siege to it for your sake.

Burgundy And where would you have been, had I withdrawn?

Talbot No worse off than at Agincourt, believe me,
when we saw off all France and you as well.

Burgundy Yet you were glad enough to have our friendship;
and the Regent paid a high enough price for it.

Talbot Yes, and today the bill fell due for payment;
disgraced, dishonoured, beaten at Orleans.

Burgundy My Lord, you may regret it if you take
this present conversation any further.
Did I desert the standards of my king,
bring down the name of traitor on my head,
to hear such language, from a foreigner?

What am I doing, fighting against my country?
If I must serve the ungrateful, I prefer
to do so for my true and lawful king.

Talbot We know you have had secret dealings with
the Dauphin, but we shall find means to shield
ourselves from treachery.

Burgundy Death and damnation!
Am I to be treated in this way?
Chatillon! See my troops prepared to march.
We shall go back to our own country.

[*Exit* CHATILLON]

Lionel Bon voyage!
The fame of Englishmen never shone so bright
as when they fought alone, with nothing but
their good stout swords, and no accomplices.
Each man should fight his battle for himself.
This demonstrates the truth of the old saying:
French blood and English don't mix well together.

[*Enter Queen* ISABEAU, *accompanied by a* PAGE]

Isabeau What am I hearing, generals? Stop this, now!
What baleful planet has disturbed your minds,
and robbed you of your senses in this way?
Will you break out in hatred at a time
when unanimity alone can save us,
and by these broils secure your own destruction?
I beg you, Duke, take back that rash command;
and Talbot, famous as you are, appease
the anger of your ally, and your friend.
Lionel, help me reconcile these fiery spirits.

Lionel Not I, my lady; it's all one to me.
In my opinion, what cannot exist
together, should much best be kept apart.

Isabeau Do the tricks of Hell, that proved so catastrophic
to us in battle, go on working here,
to fool our senses and confuse our minds?
Who began all this? Speak! My noble Lord –

[*To* TALBOT]

did you so far forget your own advantage
as to insult a valuable ally?
What do you think to gain without his aid?

He put your king upon his throne, and keeps
him there, and can remove him at his will.
His troops support your cause, his name still more so.
If every man in England landed on
our coast, they could not overcome this country
if ever it agreed to band together:
no power can conquer France, but France herself.

Talbot We know well how to honour our true friends:
to ward off false ones is a wise man's duty.

Burgundy Those who deny the debts of gratitude
are not ashamed to brazen out a lie.

Isabeau What was that, noble Duke? Can you forget
your sense of shame and honour so completely
as to extend your hand in friendship to
take the hand that cruelly killed your father?
Are you so mad as to imagine that
the Dauphin ever will be truly reconciled
with the man who drove him to the edge of ruin?
You want to pull him back, so near his fall
and thoughtlessly destroy all you have done?
Here are your friends, and your salvation rests
on alliance with England, and on that alone.

Burgundy Peace with the Dauphin had not crossed my mind;
but the contempt and arrogance displayed
by these overbearing English I won't stand.

Isabeau Come now! A rash word may be overlooked.
A general has his problems, and ill-fortune
can make a man ill-tempered, as you know.
Come on, embrace! and let me heal this rift
quickly, before it can grow any wider.

Talbot Well, Burgundy, what do you say? A noble heart
is always happy to admit the victory
of Reason's arguments. The Queen has spoken
wisely, so let this handclasp heal the wound
my over-hasty words may have inflicted.

Burgundy Madame is right in what she says. My anger,
however justified, yields to necessity.

Isabeau Good! Now seal this newly-made alliance
with a kiss of brotherhood and may the winds
carry away the words that have been spoken.

[BURGUNDY *and* TALBOT *embrace*]

Lionel [*In an undertone, observing the others*]
Much luck attend the peace made by a fury!

Isabeau Generals, we have lost one battle. Luck
was not with us, but do not, for that,
let your courage falter. If the Dauphin,
despairing of the aid of God, has called
Satanic powers into the field, he will
have sold himself to the Devil all in vain,
and Hell itself won't be enough to save him.
His army is led by this victorious girl:
I shall lead yours; I shall take the place
of prophetess and miracle-working virgin.

Lionel Madame, go back to Paris. We prefer
to fight with proper weapons, not with women.

Talbot Go! Go! Since you came to our camp,
nothing but ill-luck has attended us.

Burgundy Yes, go! You do no good by being here;
the soldiers find your presence here a scandal.

Isabeau [*Looks from one to another in astonishment*]
You too, Burgundy? Are you taking sides
against me too with these ungrateful lords?

Burgundy Just go! the men lose heart when they believe
the cause for which they're fighting might be yours.

Isabeau Scarcely have I finished making peace
between you when you're all in league against me.

Talbot Go with God, Madame, but for God's sake, go!
With you gone, we shall fear no other devils.

Isabeau But am I not your true and faithful ally?
Is not my cause the very same as yours?

Talbot Perhaps. But ours is not the same as yours.
We are engaged in an honourable war.

Burgundy And I avenge my father's bloody murder;
my cause is sanctified by filial duty.

Talbot Let us be frank! What you do to the Dauphin
cannot be justified to God nor man.

Isabeau A curse on him down to ten generations!
A man who so abuses his own mother!

Burgundy Revenge for both his father and your husband.

Isabeau Daring to sit in judgment on my morals!

Lionel Tut, tut, such lack of filial respect!

Isabeau He had me banished, sent me into exile.

Talbot In deference to what the people wanted.

Isabeau May I be damned if ever I forgive him!
Rather than have him rule his father's kingdom . . .

Talbot You'll rather sacrifice his mother's honour!

Isabeau You have no notion, poor weak souls, of what
a mother's heart, once wounded, can accomplish.
I love whoever does me good, and hate
whoever does me harm, and if it happens
that is the son I bore, I hate him worse.
I gave him life and I can take it back,
when his proud, ruthless insolence
stabs at the very womb that carried him.
You, who are fighting your war against my son,
have neither right nor reason so to rob him.
What did the Dauphin ever do to you?
What obligations has he broken to you?
Ambition and vulgar envy drive you on.
I am allowed to loathe him – he is my son.

Talbot And he can feel his mother's hand in her revenge.

Isabeau You wretched hypocrites, how I despise you.
You deceive yourselves as much as you do the world.
You English grasp out greedily for France,
where you have neither right nor valid claim
to so much earth as a horses' hoof could cover.
And this Duke, who so likes to be called "The Good",
sells off the country which his fathers left him
to foreign masters, enemies of France.
And yet, your every second word is "Justice"!
How I despise hypocrisy. The way
I am is how I want the world to see me.

Burgundy There's little danger that it won't do that.

Isabeau I have warm blood and passions like the next woman.
I came to France to be a queen, not merely
to seem one; was I to give up happiness,
because my carefree youth was cursed by Fate

to be chained to a wretched madman of a husband?
I love my freedom more than life; whoever
wounds me on that point . . . but what am I doing,
arguing about my rights – with you?
Your blood flows thick and sluggish in your veins;
of pleasure you know nothing, only rage.
And this Duke, who has wavered all his life
between the varied charms of Good and Evil,
can neither love nor hate with real conviction.
I'm going to Melun. Just let me have
this boy – I like the look of him – to keep
me company and amuse me.

[*Pointing to* LIONEL]

After that
you may do as you like. I have no further
interest in Burgundians or English.

[*She beckons to the* PAGE *and makes to go*]

Lionel Rely on us to send on to Melun
the prettiest French boys we can take prisoner.

Isabeau [*Coming back*]
You English hack away at everything in sight:
only the French can kill and still remain polite.

[*She leaves*]

Talbot God! What a woman!

Lionel Is there a decision
on whether we continue to retreat
or turn and face them, and, by a quick, bold stroke,
wipe out today's disgrace?

Burgundy No, we're too weak;
too scattered, and the men have had no time
to catch their breath after the shock they suffered.

Talbot It was blind panic, nothing else, that beat us,
the swift impression of a moment, and the image,
so frightening in imagination, seen close to,
will vanish. Therefore my advice is this,
to lead the army back at dawn tomorrow,
against the enemy.

Burgundy Consider though . . .

Lionel With your permission. There is nothing here
to be considered. We must win back all
we have lost, and soon, or be disgraced for ever.

Talbot It is decided. We attack tomorrow.
And, to destroy this phantom terror, which
so dazzles and unmans our troops, let us
engage this fiendish virgin hand-to-hand.
If she will meet us, face to face, well then,
it is the last time she will trouble us:
if not, and rest assured, she will avoid
a serious combat, then the spell is broken.

Lionel So be it then! and let me be the one
to fight this easy bloodless tournament.
I mean to take this ghost alive, and take her
personally, before the very eyes
of the Bastard Dunois, her lover, to our camp,
and let the soldiers have her.

Burgundy Do not promise
more than you can fulfil.

Talbot If ever I get
my hands on her, I shall not be so gentle.
Come now, a little sleep. We march at dawn.

[*Exeunt*]

Scene 2

[JOAN *enters, with her flag, wearing helmet and breastplate but otherwise dressed as a woman.* DUNOIS, LA HIRE, KNIGHTS *and* SOLDIERS *appear above on the cliff path, and pass silently across it, to reappear immediately afterwards on the stage*]

Joan [*To the* KNIGHTS *surrounding her, while the march past above continues*]
The pass is won, and we are in their camp!
Throw off the secret cover of the night,
which hid your silent march, and with a shout,
tell the enemy you are here in wrath,
give them our battle cry – "God and the Maid!"

All [*A loud cry with a wild clang of weapons*]
God and the Maid!

[*Trumpets and drums*]

Sentries [*Offstage*]The foe! The foe! The foe!

Joan Now bring torches! Set their tents on fire!
The fury of the flames will feed their fear,
and death will threaten them from every side.

[*The* SOLDIERS *rush off: she is about to follow them*]

Dunois [*Holding her back*]
Joan, you have done your part now. You have led us
right into their camp, delivered them
into our hand. But now you should withdraw:
leave the arbitrement of blood to us.

La Hire Point us the way to victory, and carry
the flag in front of us in your pure hand,
but do not take the sword yourself to kill,
do not tempt the treacherous god of battles,
for he is blind and merciless with his subjects.

Joan Who is there here to hold me back? And who
would dare give orders to my guiding spirit?
The arrow flies where the archer's hand directs it.
Where there is danger is where I must be.
Nor is my fate to die here, or today:
first I must see the crown on my king's head.
No enemy shall take my life until
I have fulfilled the dictates of God's will.

[*She leaves*]

La Hire Dunois! Come on then, let us follow her
and lend her all our courage for a shield.

[*Both leave*]

[*English* TROOPS *flee over the stage*]

A Soldier The maid! Here in the camp!

Another Impossible!
How can she be? How can she have got in?

Another Through the air. The Devil helped her.

Two More Run! Run! We're dead men, all of us.

[*Exeunt*]

Talbot [*Entering*] They will not hear. I cannot rally them.
All discipline has left them; just as if
the legions of the damned had been spewed out
of Hell, a panic has swept both coward and hero
senselessly off. I cannot find ten men

to throw against the enemy, who floods
into the camp in ever-increasing force.
Am I the only sober man, and all
the rest are raving lunatics? To fly
before these milksop Frenchies, whom we have
trounced in a dozen battles? Who is she,
this invincible goddess of terror, who can turn
the tide of battle all at once, and change
a flock of sheep into a pride of lions?
Could an impostor learn a leading part
so well that she could terrify real heroes?

A Soldier [*Rushing in*] General! The Maid! Run!

Talbot [*Strikes him down*]
Run yourself!
To Hell! And any man who speaks of flight
or fear shall have to reckon with my sword.

[*He goes out. The scene opens out till we see the English camp in flames. Drums, flight and pursuit. After a little while, enter* MONTGOMERY]

Montgomery Where shall I run to? Death and enemies surround me.
The furious general brandishes his sword to block
our flight and drive us to our deaths, on one side, while
upon the other, she, the terrible Maid, deals death
and rages like a fire! And not a bush to hide me,
not a cave to offer me a place of safety!
Why did I ever have to come across the sea,
miserable fool! I was deceived by an illusion,
to look for cheap and easy fame in the war in France.
Now my ill-luck has brought me to this bloody battle.
I wish I was a long, long way from here, at home,
on the Severn's flowery banks, safe in my father's house,
where I left my mother, weeping, and my girl.

[JOAN *appears in the distance*]

Oh, God! what do I see! She's there, the horror's coming!
Rising, glowing darkly, out of the flames of fire,
like a spirit of the night, out of the jaws of Hell.
Where can I run away to? She holds me in her eyes
of fire already, casting out her net of glances,
unerringly, towards me from far off. My feet
are caught in her snares, tighter and ever tighter,
they refuse to carry me. However much my heart
misgives, I have to look upon that face of death.

[JOAN *takes a few steps towards him, and stops again*]

She's coming nearer. I'll not wait until the fiend
attacks me first. I shall go on my knees to her,
beg her, implore her for my life – she is a woman –
I have to see if tears have any power to move her.

[*As he starts to go towards her, she advances on him quickly*]

Joan You are a dead man! You were born of an English mother.

Montgomery [*Falling at her feet*]
No! Stop! You cannot murder a defenceless man.
I threw away my sword and shield. I am unarmed,
and begging you, falling at your feet, for mercy.
Leave me the light of life, and take a ransom fee.
My father is a rich man, he has property at home,
in Wales, that lovely country, where the silver Severn
snakes through green fields, and fifty villages acknowledge
him as their lord. He will send gold, much gold, to free
a son he loves, if he finds out I'm still alive,
a prisoner of the French.

Joan You lost, deluded fool!
You've fallen in the fatal hands of Joan the Maid,
from whom no rescue or escape can be expected.
If Fate had placed you in the power of the tiger,
the crocodile, if you had robbed a lioness of
her cubs, you might have found some pity or compassion.
But there is one way only, for those who meet the Maid.
A terrible contract binds me to the spirit-world,
powerful, invulnerable, and enjoins me
to put to the sword and slaughter every living thing
sent fatally against me by the god of battles.

Montgomery Oh, what you say is terrible, but your looks are mild.
You are not frightening at all seen nearer to.
My heart is drawn to you, you are so beautiful.
Oh, by the mildness of your tender sex, I beg you:
have mercy! I am young.

Joan Do not invoke my sex!
Do not call me a woman! I have no sex. Like spirits
bodiless, not subjected to the world's ways of loving,
I have no sex, nor does this armour hide a heart.

Montgomery Oh, by the holy ruling power of love, which every
heart is subject to, I beg you now to hear me.
I left behind at home, the girl who was to be

my wife, lovely as you, fresh in the charm of youth,
weeping and waiting for her lover to come back.
Oh, if you ever hope to be in love, and hope
your love will be returned, then do not cruelly
divide two hearts that feel the sacred bonds of love.

Joan You call upon the alien gods of Earth, whom I
neither worship nor respect. And I know nothing
of all these sacred bonds of love you tell me of;
nor shall I ever recognise its idle power.
Therefore defend yourself; your last hour is at hand.

Montgomery Oh, then have mercy on my sorrowing parents, whom
I left behind at home. For you, too, must have parents,
left, sick with worry and concern for you.

Joan That was unlucky to remind me of how many
mothers have been made childless here in France,
how many helpless children fatherless, how many
promised brides have been made widows, and through you!
Now let English women experience despair,
and learn to know the tears that have been shed
by France's sorrow-stricken wives and mothers.

Montgomery It is hard to die unmourned, and in a foreign land.

Joan Who asked you to that land, to lay waste to the crops,
growing in our fields, to drive us from our homes,
to throw the firebrand of war into the peace
and sanctity of our cities? You cherished the illusion
you could reduce the free-born French to abject slavery;
that you could harness this great country, like a dinghy,
behind your mighty man-of-war. Well, you are fools!
The royal arms of France hang near the throne of God:
and you will sooner snatch a star from the Great Bear,
than a village from this country, for it stands eternal,
united, indivisible. The day of vengeance
is near at hand; and you shall not return alive
across that sacred channel God has placed to set
a frontier between our countries, and which you
have blasphemously overstepped.

Montgomery Oh, I must die!
Death's terror seizes me already.

Joan Die, then, friend!
Why timidly draw back from Death, which is the fate
none of us may avoid? Look at me, now. Look!

I am nothing but a girl, a shepherdess by birth,
these hands of mine are quite unused to hold a sword,
they never carried anything more harmful than a crook;
yet, torn away from all the places of my homeland,
my father's arms, my sisters', I must here, I must –
the voice of Heaven drives me on, not my own will –
rage like an angry spirit, to do you bitter harm,
no joy to me, dealing out death, and at the last,
falling myself a victim to him. I shall not
see the day when I come home again in joy.
I shall bring death to many of you yet, I shall
make many widows still, but, finally, I shall
be killed myself, and so I shall fulfil my destiny.
Now you must fulfil yours. Take up your sword again,
and we shall fight together for the prize of life.

Montgomery [*Standing*] If you are mortal like myself, if weapons can
wound you, perhaps it is my arm that is predestined
to send you down to Hell, and end the woes of England.
I lay my fate in God's all-merciful hand. Now, witch!
Call up your devils to your aid! Fight for your life!

[*He snatches up his sword and shield and attacks her: military music sounds in the distance: after a short struggle,* MONTGOMERY *falls*]

Joan Your foot was set upon the road to Death – then go there!

[*She moves away from him, and stands, thoughtfully*]

Oh, Blessed Virgin, you have worked a miracle in me!
You give the strength to my unwarlike arm, and arm
this heart of mine with stern implacability.
My soul melts into pity and my hand draws back,
as if it was encroaching on some holy shrine,
from violating the young bodies of my foes.
I shudder at the very sight of naked steel,
but when the need is there, there also is the strength,
and in my trembling hand, the sword unerringly
moves of its own accord, as if it were alive.

[*Enter a* KNIGHT *with closed visor*]

Knight Damned juggling witch! Your hour has come. All over
the field of battle I have looked for you.
Devil, go back now to the Hell you came from.

Joan What man are you, his evil angel sends
to meet me? By your bearing, you could be
a prince; nor do you seem an Englishman,
you wear the insignia of Burgundy,
and against those I shall not raise my sword.

Knight Degenerate wretch! You do not merit death
at a prince's noble hand. The headsman's axe
should sever your damned head from off your body,
and not the royal sword of Burgundy.

Joan So then you are the noble Duke himself?

Knight [*Raising his visor*]
I am! Wretched creature, tremble and despair!
your hellish tricks will not protect you now.
Till now you only had to deal with weaklings;
this is a man who faces you.

Dunois [*Entering with* LA HIRE]
Then turn
and fight with men, not women, Burgundy.

La Hire We shall protect the holy prophetess:
your sword will have to run me through before . . .

Burgundy This ruttish sorceress does not frighten me,
and nor do you, whom she has changed so vilely.
You should blush, Bastard, and you too, La Hire,
for lowering your one-time valour to
the arts of Hell, letting yourselves become
the paltry squires of a devil's trull.
Come on! I challenge all of you. The man
who seeks the aid of Hell, despairs of God.

[*They prepare to fight.* JOAN *steps in between them*]

Joan Stop!

Burgundy Are you frightened for your lover's life?
Before your very eyes, he shall be . . .
[*He lunges at* DUNOIS]

Joan Stop!
Part them, La Hire. No French blood must be spilt.
It is not swords that must decide this quarrel.
It has been otherwise decreed above.
Stand apart, I say! Hear and revere
the spirit that enters me, and speaks through me.

Dunois Why do you stay my upraised arm, and why
prevent my sword from settling this in blood?
The steel is drawn, the blow must fall that brings
vengeance and reconciliation to all France .

Joan [*Standing between them, and dividing both parties by a wide space, speaks to the* BASTARD]
Stand over there.

[*To* LA HIRE]

Don't move from where you are.
I must speak to the Duke.

[*When everyone is quiet*]

Well, Burgundy?
What is it that you want? Who are these foes
whom you look for with murder in your eyes?
This noble prince is a son of France like you,
this brave man is your countryman and brother
in arms, and I myself a daughter of
your nation. All of us, whom you are trying
to wipe out, we are all one people – yours.
Our arms are spread wide open to receive you;
our knees will gladly bend to do you homage;
our swords will not be raised against you, since
even in enemy uniform, we respect
the royal features we can see in you.

Burgundy Siren! do you intend to lure your victim
with flattery and sweet words to destruction?
Your tricks cannot impose on me. My ears
are stopped to the seductions of your speech,
the armour on my breast is proof against
the fiery arrows darting from your eyes.
Dunois, to arms!
And let us fight with weapons, not with words.

Dunois Words first, then blows. Are you afraid of words?
That is a sort of cowardice as well,
betraying a lack of confidence in your cause.

Joan We are not forced to kneel here at your feet.
We do not come to you as suppliants.
Look around! The English camp is burned,
your dead are covering the battlefield,
the drums that you hear beating are French drums:

God has decided, victory is ours.
We are prepared to share the laurels, though,
freshly-plucked as they are, with our friend.
Come over to us! An honourable flight!
Come over to the side of right and victory.
I, who am sent by God, I offer you
a sister's hand, to draw you over to
the side of justice: I shall save you yet.
Heaven sides with France. The angelic host –
although you cannot see them – fight for our King;
the fleur de lys adorns them; like this flag,
our cause is good, and white as purest light;
and its chaste symbol is the Blessed Virgin.

Burgundy The tangled web of lies snares and deceives,
but her speech is just as artless as a child's.
If evil spirits prompt her, they have done
a wonderful counterfeit of innocence.
I will not listen any more. To arms!
I feel my ear is weaker than my hand.

Joan You say I am a sorceress, and accuse me
of devil's tricks – is making peace a trick?
disarming hatred an affair of Hell?
Does harmony rise from the infernal regions?
If anything is innocent, good and holy,
is it not surely fighting for one's country?
Since when has Nature been so much at odds
with herself that Heaven would desert
the cause of Right, and devils would defend it?
But if what I have said to you is good,
where would I have it from if not from Heaven?
Who would have to come to me among my flocks,
to teach a simple girl affairs of state?
Princes and kings were strangers to my eyes,
as arts of speech are foreign to my tongue.
But now I need them to convince you, I
possess the insight into higher things.
The fate of kings and empires is now clear
as daylight to my calm, unclouded eyes,
and in my mouth I bear a thunderbolt.

Burgundy [*Deeply agitated, raises his eyes to her, and looks at her with astonishment and emotion*]
What's happening to me? Is it a god

that brings about this change of heart in me?
She is not false, if she can move me so.
No! No! If it is magic works on me,
it is the working of a heavenly power;
my heart tells me – she has been sent from God.

Joan Look! He is moved! He is! I have not begged
in vain. The thundercloud of anger melts,
and thaws in tears, and from his eyes there shines
the light of peace, the sunlight of emotion.
Put up your swords, and take him to your hearts.
He weeps, we have convinced him, he is ours!

[*Her sword and flag fall from her hands, she hurries over to him with arms outstretched, and embraces him with passionate intensity.* LA HIRE *and* DUNOIS *lower their swords, and hasten over to embrace him*]

Act 3

Scene 1

[*The court at Chalons-sur-Marne*]

Dunois We have been bosom friends, comrades in arms;
drawing our swords in common cause, and in
adversity and death we stayed together.
Don't let a woman break the bond that has
outlasted every twist and turn of Fate.

La Hire Prince, listen . . .

Dunois La Hire! You are in love with Joan.
I know quite well what you intend to do:
to go at once to the King and ask him for
her hand as a reward – he hardly can
refuse your bravery what it deserves.
But hear this – rather than see her in the arms
of someone else, I would . . .

La Hire Prince, let me speak!

Dunois It's not the superficial pleasure of
the eye that draws me to her. I had never
been attracted by a woman; then I saw her,
the miracle-working girl whom God had sent
to save the country and to be my wife.
That was the moment when I swore by all
that I hold sacred, I would marry her.
None but the strong deserve the strong: my heart
burns with a longing to find rest upon
a kindred bosom which both understands
and can stand up to all its strength and power.

La Hire I would never dare to weigh my poor deserts
against the power of your heroic name.
When Count Dunois enters the lists, then all
the competition may as well withdraw.
But can a low-born shepherdess be worthy
to sit beside you as a wife? Would not
the royal blood that flows in your veins
disdain to be so shamefully diluted?

Dunois She is a child of God and Nature, just
as I am, and therefore of equal birth.
How could she disgrace a Prince's hand,
she who is wedded to the holy angels,
whose head is haloed with a brighter crown
than any on this earth, who sees the pomp
and circumstance of the world as dross beneath
her feet; pile all the thrones of all the kings
of all the earth on one another, till
they reach the stars, they would not reach the heights
where she reigns in angelic majesty!

La Hire Then let the King decide.

Dunois No! She must choose!
She has freed France, she must be free to give
her heart.

La Hire The King!

[*Enter* CHARLES, SOREL, DU CHATEL, CHATILLON *and the* ARCHBISHOP]

Charles You say he's coming here?
To recognise me as his rightful king?

Chatillon Here, Sire, in your royal city of Chalons,
the Duke, my master, means to throw himself
in penance at your feet – he ordered me
to greet Your Majesty as lord and king:
and say he follows and will soon be here.

Sorel He's coming! Oh, the brightness of this day
that brings joy, peace, and reconciliation!

Chatillon My Lord will bring two hundred knights with him;
he will kneel down in homage at your feet.
However, he expects that you will not
permit that, but will greet him as your cousin.

Charles My heart burns to beat in time with his.

Chatillon The Duke requests no mention shall be made
of the old feud at this, your first, encounter.

Charles The past shall be forgotten, and for ever.
We only wish the future to be bright.

Chatillon Those who have fought for Burgundy shall be
included in the general amnesty.

Charles In that way I gain twice as many subjects.

Chatillon Queen Isabeau shall also be included
in this agreement, should she wish to accept it.

Charles She wages war on me, not I on her:
our fight is over, as soon as she likes to end it.

Chatillon Twelve knights shall be hostages for your word.

Charles My word is sacred.

Chatillon The Archbishop shall
divide a sacred host between you both,
as pledge and seal of reconciliation.

Charles As I hope for salvation at the last,
my heart and hand are both at one in this.
What other pledges does the Duke require?

Chatillon [*With a glance at* DU CHATEL]
There is one person here, whose presence might
sour the first greeting.

[DU CHATEL *walks silently away*]

Charles Go, then, Du Chatel:
stay hidden till the Duke can bear to see you.

[*He follows him with his eyes, then hurries over to him, and embraces him*]

My honest friend, you have been more than ready
to do this and much more to save my peace!

[DU CHATEL *leaves*]

Chatillon This document explains the other points.

Charles [*To the* ARCHBISHOP]
See it is all arranged. We shall agree
to everything – no price too high for a friend.
Dunois! take a hundred knights and go
to meet the Duke and bring him here in friendship.
The troops must have green branches in their helmets
to greet their brothers; and the city must
be decorated for a festival,
and all the bells shall ring to announce the news
that France and Burgundy are reconciled.

[*Enter a* PAGE. *Trumpets heard off*]

Listen! What is the meaning of those fanfares?

Page The Duke of Burgundy has made his entrance
into the court.

[*Exit*]

Dunois [*Going out with* LA HIRE *and* CHATILLON]
Come! Let us go to meet him.

Charles [*To* SOREL] Agnès, you're crying? I too barely have
the strength to take me through this interview.
How many had to die to make it possible
for us to meet in friendship once again!
But every tempest spends itself at last,
day follows even the darkest night, and time
brings ripeness to even the latest fruits.

Archbishop [*At the window*]
The Duke can hardly force a passage through
the mob. They've lifted him from off his horse,
kissing his cloak, his spurs.

Charles A kindly people,
their love flares up as quickly as their anger.
They soon forget it was this very Duke
who massacred their fathers and their sons:
one moment swallows up a lot of time!
– Control yourself, Agnès! Excess of joy
might also prove a thorn in the flesh: I want
nothing to cause him shame or bitterness.

[*Enter the Duke of* BURGUNDY, DUNOIS, LA HIRE, CHATILLON, *and two other* KNIGHTS *of the Duke's entourage.* BURGUNDY *stops at the entrance; the* KING *goes towards him; at the same time,* BURGUNDY *comes forward, and, just as he is about to kneel,* CHARLES *takes him in his arms*]

You have surprised us – we had meant to come
to meet you – but you have the faster horses.

Burgundy Bearing me to my duty.

[*He embraces* SOREL, *kissing her on the forehead*]

By your leave,
cousin: this is the lord's privilege
at Arras, and no pretty woman dares
oppose the custom.

Charles We are told your court
is the seat of Love, the market-place as well,
where all things beautiful are kept in stock.

Burgundy Your Majesty, we are a trading nation,
all that is rich and pleasant from all lands,
comes to the market-place at Bruges to be

displayed for show and use: in value, though,
nothing exceeds the beauty of our women.

Sorel Surely their fidelity should have
a higher value, if not in the market.

Charles You have a wicked, libellous reputation,
for taking woman's virtue lightly, cousin.

Burgundy Heresy is its own worst punishment.
You are a lucky man, my liege. Your heart
has taught you early, what a dissolute life
has taught me late.

[*He sees the* ARCHBISHOP, *and gives him his hand*]

Your blessing, Monseigneur.
In the right place, as ever. He who wants
to find you, needs to tread the path of virtue.

Archbishop Now let my Maker call me when He will:
my heart is full of joy, I can depart
in peace now, since my eyes have seen this day!

Burgundy [*To* SOREL] They say you robbed yourself of all your jewels
to furnish arms against me. Is it true?
Are you so warlike? Was your mind so bent
on my destruction? But our war is over,
all that was lost is found again. Your jewels
have also found their way back to their owner.
You gave them up to ruin me in war:
now take them from my hand, in sign of peace.

[*From one of his attendants he takes a jewel casket and presents it to her, opened.* SOREL *looks at the* KING *in amazement*]

Charles Take it: a doubly precious gift, a pledge
of love to me and reconciliation.

Burgundy [*Fixing a jewelled rose in* SOREL*'s hair*]
Why is this not the royal crown of France?
My heart would feel an equal joy to place it
on such a beautiful head.

[*Taking her hand, significantly*]

Rely on me,
if ever you should need a friend!

[SOREL *bursts into tears and steps aside: the* KING *also struggles to control his feelings: all present watch the two* PRINCES *with emotion.* BURGUNDY, *after looking round the whole circle, finally throws himself into the* KING*'s embrace*]

Oh, my dear king!

[*At the same moment, the three Burgundian* KNIGHTS *hurry forward to embrace* DUNOIS, LA HIRE *and the* ARCHBISHOP. *Both* PRINCES *stand for some time without speaking, in each other's arms*]

How could I have hated you? How could I
have abandoned you?

Charles Come now, be still, no more.

Burgundy How could I crown that Englishman, and swear
an oath of loyalty to a foreigner!
and all of this to bring about your ruin!

Charles Forget the past! All is forgiven. All
blotted out in a single moment! It
was Destiny, or some unlucky star.

Burgundy [*Grasping his hand*]
I shall right this wrong: believe me, I shall!
Make reparation for all you have suffered.
Your kingdom shall be given back to you
entire – not a village will be missing!

Charles We are agreed. I fear no other foe.

Burgundy Believe me, it was with a heavy heart
I took up arms against you. If you knew . . .
Why did you never send this lady to me?

[*Pointing to* SOREL]

Those tears of hers I could not have resisted.
No power of Hell can separate us now,
not since we have embraced in brotherhood.
Now I have found out where I need to be,
on this heart all my wanderings have an end.

Archbishop [*Stepping between them*]
Princes, you are united! France arises,
phoenix-like from her ashes, giving promise
of a bright future. The land's grievous wounds
will heal: the villages, the towns that were
destroyed, will rise more splendid from the rubble:
the fields will once again be green. But those
who were the victims of your fatal quarrel,
the dead, will not rise up again: the tears

that have been shed for them cannot be unshed.
The coming generation will be blessed, but not
the one that was the quarry of disaster.
The children's happiness will not wake their fathers.
These are the fruits of war between two brothers!
And let this prove a lesson: fear the god
that dwells within the sword, before you draw it.
The hand of the mighty may unleash a war:
the savage god, though, is not trained to come
like a falcon, back from the skies to the hunter's hand –
he will not come when called. The hand of Heaven
will not save us so punctually twice.

Burgundy My liege! You have an angel by your side.
Where is she? Why do I not see her here?

Charles Where is Joan? Why is she not with us now,
in this high, solemn hour that she made possible?

Archbishop She does not like the life of ease at court,
Your Majesty, and when divine command
does not call her to stand before the world,
she modestly avoids the vulgar gaze.
She is certainly in communion with God,
unless she is labouring for France's good,
for Heaven's blessing attends all her footsteps.

[*Enter* JOAN, *in armour, but without a helmet, wearing a wreath in her hair*]

Charles Joan, you appear like a priestess. Have you come
to consecrate the friendship you began?

Burgundy How frightening she was in battle, and
how peace surrounds her with a shining grace!
– Joan! Have I kept my word? Are you content?
Do I not merit your approval now?

Joan The greatest good you did was to yourself.
You are now all arrayed in blessed light,
where before all was a gloomy, blood-red glow,
hung like a moon of terror in the sky.

[*She looks about*]

I see assembled here a number of
noble knights, whose eyes all shine with joy,
only one sorrowful one have I encountered,
who has to hide himself, while all rejoice.

Burgundy And who is conscious of such heavy guilt
that he despairs of winning our goodwill?

Joan May he approach? Oh, tell me that he may!
Make your reform complete. It cannot be
called reconciliation, where the heart
is not entirely freed. One drop of hatred
left in the cup of joy turns all to poison.
However black the crime, let Burgundy
forgive it on this day of celebration.

Burgundy Your drift is getting clearer.

Joan Will you forgive him?
You will, Duke? – Come in, Du Chatel!

[*She opens the door and leads in* DU CHATEL, *who stops some distance away*]

The Duke is reconciled to all his enemies,
you too.

Burgundy What are you doing to me, Joan?
Are you aware of what it is you're asking?

Joan A generous master opens his doors to all,
there is no guest that he shuts out. A pardon,
free as the firmament above the earth,
should not distinguish between friend and foe.
The sun's rays are sent out alike to each
and every corner of infinity;
the sky drops dew in equal measure on
all living things that thirst. All that is good,
all that comes from above belongs to all,
without reserve: but darkness dwells in corners.

Burgundy Oh, she can twist and bend me as she pleases.
My heart turns to soft putty in her hands.
– Du Chatel! Come! Embrace me. I forgive you.
Ghost of my father, do not scold, if I
now take in friendship the hand that struck you down.
Gods of death, do not hold it against me,
if I now break my solemn vow of vengeance.
Down in your home of everlasting night,
no heart beats any more; all is eternal,
fixed, motionless. But up here,in the sunlight,
it is different: Man lives, and feels, and is
the easy prey of the tremendous moment.

Charles [*To* JOAN] What is there I do not have you to thank for?
Marvellous girl! How well you kept your word!
How quickly you reversed my destiny,
reconciled me with my friends, and threw
my enemies down into the dust, and freed
my cities from the foreign yoke! You alone
accomplished this. How am I to reward you?

Joan Be as humane in your prosperity
as in adversity – and on the summit
remember the value of a friend in need,
which you have learned in times of degradation.
Do not refuse the meanest of your subjects
justice and mercy; it was from the sheepfolds
that God called your deliverer. You will
unite all France beneath your rule, and be
the father of a mighty line of kings;
those who come after you shall shine more brightly
than those who have preceded you on the throne.
The line will flourish, just as long as it
retains the love its people feel for it.
All that can bring it to a fall is pride:
from the mean huts from which salvation came
to you today, mysterious destruction
threatens the guilty scions of your house.

Burgundy You whom the voice of Heaven inspires to prophecy,
if you can see into the womb of time,
speak to me also of my dynasty. Will it
continue in the splendour it began in?

Joan Duke, you have raised your seat as high as a throne,
and your proud heart would raise it higher still,
to lift the whole bold structure to the clouds.
But a higher power will suddenly halt its growth.
Do not for that, though, fear your houses' fall.
It will live on in splendour through a daughter,
and sceptred kings, the shepherds of their people,
will issue from her. They shall sit upon
twin thrones of power, and hand down laws to all
the known world, and to another, newer world,
that God still hides across uncharted seas.

Charles Tell us, now, if the Spirit will reveal it,
will this alliance we have just renewed,
also unite our children and grandchildren?

Joan [*After a pause*]
You – Kings and rulers! Have a care of discord!
Do not wake the spirit of dissension,
now sleeping in its lair, for, once aroused,
it will not easily be tamed again.
It will beget a brood of iron children,
and from one firebrand, light one after another.
– Demand to know no further, but enjoy
the present, while I silently conceal
the shape of things to come.

Sorel Oh, holy maid,
you see into my heart. You know if it
is vainly seeking greatness. Give me too
a welcome prophecy.

Joan The spirit shows
me only the mighty happenings in the world.
Your destiny is contained in your own breast.

Dunois Exalted and beloved of God, what will
your destiny be? All happiness on earth
should be hers, who is holiness itself.

Joan Happiness dwells with my eternal Father.

Charles Your happiness is henceforth your king's concern:
for I shall make your name great through all France,
all future generations shall call thee blessed.
This shall be done at once! Kneel down!

[*He draws his sword and touches her with it*]

Now, rise:
a noblewoman! I, your king, here raise you
out of the dust of your obscure birth –
your forbears I ennoble in their graves –
your coat of arms shall bear the fleur-de-lys,
and you shall be the equal of the best
in France: none but the blood of Valois shall
be held superior to yours. The greatest
of all my subjects shall feel honoured by
your hand, and it shall be my first concern
to fit you with a worthy, noble husband.

Dunois [*Stepping forward*]
My heart chose her already, when she was
nothing: this latest honour does her justice,
but changes neither her merits or my love.

Here in the presence of my sovereign and
this holy bishop, I do offer her
my hand, to be my noble consort, if
she thinks me worthy to make such an offer.

Charles Wonder on wonder! Now I must believe
that nothing is impossible to you:
if you can bring this stubborn heart to heel,
which always scorned the universal power
of Love, until this moment.

La Hire [*Stepping forward*]
But her brightest
ornament, if I understand her right,
is modesty of heart. She well deserves
the homage of the great, but she will never
raise her desires so high. She does not strive
to reach the dizzy peaks of earthly grandeur.
She is contented with the true affection
of an honest heart, and with the tranquil lot
which I here offer to her, with my hand.

Charles La Hire, you as well! Two noble claimants,
one famous and heroic as the other!
You reconcile my enemies, unite
my kingdom, now you want to part my friends?
Well, only one of them can have her: since
in my judgment, both are worthy of her,
then she must speak herself, her heart must choose.

Sorel [*Coming closer*] The noble maid is taken by surprise,
I see the blood rush to her modest cheeks.
Let her have time to ask her heart the question:
unburden herself to a friend of her own sex,
and break the seal still on her tight-locked breast.
Now is the moment even I may be
allowed to go to this unbending girl,
and offer her the confidence of a sister.
Let women first talk over womens' matters,
and wait and see what we decide.

Charles So be it!

[*He starts to leave*]

Joan No! Sire, not so! The reason why I blushed
was not the confusion of some silly shame.
I've nothing to confide to this great lady

I'd be ashamed to say in front of men.
These noble men have honoured me in their choice,
but I did not give up a shepherd's life, to gain
an empty, high position in the world.
Nor did I put on armour, so that I
could braid a bridal wreath into my hair.
It is a different mission I am called to,
and one which only a virgin can complete.
I am a soldier of the Lord of Hosts:
I cannot be the wife of any man.

Archbishop Woman was made for man, to be his loving
companion, and she best serves the will
of God, if she obeys the voice of Nature.
When you have carried out sufficiently
your God's commands upon the battlefield,
then you will lay aside your arms and come
back to the gentler sex you have denied,
unsuited to the bloody work of war.

Joan Most reverend Father, I cannot yet say
what the Spirit will order me to do:
but when the time comes, it will not be silent,
and I shall do its bidding. For the moment,
it bids me to complete my work. My Lord
is not yet crowned: the sacred oil has not
been poured upon his head, nor does my Lord
yet bear the title of the King of France.

Charles Our feet are set upon the road to Rheims.

Joan We cannot loiter while the enemy
is still on the alert to intercept us.
But I shall lead you on through all of them!

Dunois But when it is all over, and complete,
when we have entered Rheims victorious,
then, oh, most holy maiden, will you let me . . .

Joan If it is Heaven's will that I come back
victorious, from this mortal struggle, then
my work will be done – the shepherdess will have
no further business in her sovereign's house.

Charles [*Taking her hand*]
It is the Spirit's voice that moves you now,
silencing Love in the heart that God has filled.
But believe me, it will not be quiet for ever!

Weapons will be laid aside, and victory
will lead Peace by the hand, and joy return
to every heart, and gentler feelings wake
in every breast – in yours as well – and you
will shed tears of sweet unfulfilled desire,
such as you never shed before: that heart
which Heaven alone now fills to overflowing,
will turn in love towards a mortal lover.
Your rescuing arm has rendered thousands happy:
you will, at last, bring happiness to one.

Joan Dauphin! Are you so tired already of
the visible presence of God, you seek to smash
the vessel that contains it, and drag down
into the dust, the virgin God has sent you?
Oh, ye of little faith! Your hearts are blind!
The majesty of Heaven shines around you:
its miracles are done before your eyes:
and you see nothing in me but a woman.
Well, is it womanly to strap on armour
and meddle in the male preserve of war?
And woe betide me if I took God's sword
of vengeance in my hand, while in my heart
I bore an idle passion for some man!
Better for me, if I had not been born!
Not one word more of this, I tell you, if
you do not wish to see the spirit in me
roused to a fury. Any man who looks
at me with longing is a horror to me,
a sacrilege.

Charles Enough! There is no point in trying to move her.

Joan Give the command to sound for the attack.
This cease-fire frightens and depresses me;
it rouses me out of this idle rest,
to see my mission done, recalling me
to put my destiny to the final test.

[*Enter a* KNIGHT *in haste*]

Charles What is it?

Knight The enemy has crossed the Marne,
and drawn his army up in line of battle.

Joan Battle and War! Now my soul's fetters fall.
To arms! I shall see the army marshalled.

[*She hurries out*]

Charles La Hire, go with her – they mean to make us fight
for the crown to the gates of Rheims itself.

Dunois It is not real courage drives them, but
the last throw of a frantic, faint despair.

Charles I do not spur you, cousin Burgundy.
Today atones for many evil days.

Burgundy You will have no complaint of me.

Charles I shall
march at your head along the road to glory,
and at the coronation city, fight
for a crown. – Agnès! your knight bids you farewell.

Sorel [*Embraces him*]
I shall not weep for you, nor tremble for you.
My faith is firmly placed up in the clouds;
So many signs and pledges of Heaven's grace
are not vouchsafed to end in grief and pain.
My conquering lord I shall again embrace
– my heart tells me – when Rheims is ours again!

[*Trumpets sound an energetic flourish, which changes, during the scene-change, to wild, discordant battle-music. As the next scene starts, the music strikes up, accompanied by an off-stage military band*]

Scene 2

[*The scene changes to an open space, bordered by trees. During the opening music,* SOLDIERS *can be seen, swiftly retreating in the background*]

[TALBOT *enters, leaning on* FASTOLF, *accompanied by* SOLDIERS]

Talbot Put me down here now, underneath these trees,
and take yourselves back to the battle. I
do not need anybody's help to die.

Fastolf This is a terrible, unhappy day!

[*Enter* LIONEL]

Oh, what a sight you find here, Lionel:
the general is mortally wounded.

Lionel God forbid!
My Lord, stand up, this is no time for weakness.
Do not give in to Death, use your iron will
to order Nature to revive in you!

Talbot No use! The day has come when it is fated
that we should lose the throne we held in France.
I have staked our last strength in a desperate fight
to avert this fate, but it has been in vain.
And I lie here, struck to the ground by steel,
I shall not rise again – and Rheims is lost;
now hurry to save Paris.

Lionel Paris has signed a treaty with the Dauphin:
a courier came just now bringing the news.

Talbot [*Tearing off his bandages*]
Then let the rivers of my blood flood out,
for I am tired of looking at this sun.

Lionel I cannot stay here – Fastolf, take the general
to somewhere safe, we cannot hold our present
position: the men are flying on all sides.
The Maid is pressing forward, unopposed.

Talbot The triumph of folly, and the death of me!
With idiocy the gods themselves contend
in vain. Reason, exalted, and sublime,
bright-rayed daughter, sprung from the head of God,
the wise ordainer of the universe,
the steerer of the stars, who are you then,
when, tied to the tail of the maddened horse of Frenzy,
calling out unavailingly, you see
yourselves hurled down together to the pit?
Damn all of those who spend their lives pursuing
the great, the worthy, and whose noble minds
are spent in well-laid plans. The King of Fools
is lord of this world . . .

Lionel General, you have
not much time left – think of your Maker now!

Talbot If we had been brave men, and had been beaten
by other brave men, we could have found comfort
in the common fate of all men, and the turns
of Fortune on her wheel – but to have been
conquered by such vulgar conjuring tricks!
Was all our serious and hard-working life
not worthy of a more imposing exit?

Lionel [*Giving him his hand*]
My lord, goodbye. The tears I owe you shall
be paid in full after the battle's over,
assuming I am still alive to pay them.
But now the fate that sits above the field
in judgment, handing down men's destinies,
summons me too. We meet in another world:
so short a parting for so long a friendship.

[*He goes out*]

Talbot Soon it will all be over; I shall give
back to the earth, the everlasting sun,
those atoms which made up my joy and sorrow –
and of the mighty soldier Talbot, whose
great fame once filled the world, there will be nothing
but a little handful of dust – so a man dies.
And all the profit we can reap from this
struggle of life is insight into . . . nothing,
and cordial contempt for everything
that we thought noble and desirable . . .

[*Enter* CHARLES, BURGUNDY, DUNOIS, DU CHATEL, *and* TROOPS]

Burgundy We have taken the redoubt.

Dunois The day is ours.

Charles [*Noticing* TALBOT]
See who that is over there who bids so hard
and unwilling a farewell to the light of day?
His armour shows he is no common soldier.
Give him some help, if help is still to give.

[SOLDIERS *step forward*]

Fastolf Get back! And stand away! Respect the death
of a man you never came near when alive.

Burgundy What do I see? Talbot, covered in blood!

[*He goes towards him.* TALBOT *stares at him unblinkingly and dies*]

Fastolf Get away, Burgundy! A hero's dying eyes
should not be pained by looking at a traitor!

Dunois The Talbot we so feared! The invincible!
Are you content with such a little ground
for whom the whole of France was not enough
to satisfy your spirit's great ambition?
Now, for the first time, Sire, I call you King,

the crown still sat uneasily on your head
as long as there was still breath in this body.

Charles [*After looking silently at the dead man*]
A higher power has struck him down, not we.
He lies upon the soil of France, just like
a hero on the shield he would not leave.
Take him away!

[SOLDIERS *lift the corpse and carry it out*]

And peace be with his dust!
He shall be given a monument of honour.
Here, in the midst of France, where his career
as hero ended, there his bones will rest.
No enemy advanced as far as he;
the place he died shall be his epitaph.

Fastolf [*Giving up his sword*]
My Lord, I am your prisoner.

Charles [*Giving it back*]
Not at all!
Such duties are respected even in war.
Follow your master to the grave in freedom.
Du Chatel, hurry to Agnès, relieve her
of the anxiety with which she trembles for us.
Tell her we are victorious and alive,
bring her to Rheims in triumph!

[*Enter* LA HIRE]

Dunois La Hire!
Where is the Maid?

La Hire I might ask that of you.
I left her fighting at your side.

Dunois I thought
she was protected by your troops, when I
hurried away to give the King assistance.

Burgundy I saw her banner waving in the thick
of the enemy forces not so long ago.

Dunois Oh, God, where is she? I feel a foreboding
of ill. Come, we must save her. I'm afraid
her courage may have taken her too far,
and that she fights alone, hemmed in all round,
she may fall victim to sheer weight of numbers.

Charles Save her!

La Hire I am with you.

Burgundy So are we all!

[*They rush out*]

Scene 3

[*Another desolate part of the battlefield. In the distance, the towers of Rheims can be seen in the sunlight*]

[*A* KNIGHT *appears, entirely in black armour, with a closed visor.* JOAN *pursues him to the front of the stage, where he halts and stands, waiting for her*]

Joan Creature of tricks! I can see through them now.
Deceitfully, by counterfeited flight
you have enticed me from the battlefield,
saving so many British boys from death and destiny.
But fate has finally caught up with you.

The Black Knight
Why do you dog me in this way, and cling
so furiously to my heels? It is not
your hand by which it is my fate to die.

Joan I hate you from the bottom of my soul,
creature of night, whose colour is your own
An overmastering desire impels me
to blot you out utterly from the light of day.
Who are you? Put your visor up. Had I
not seen the warlike Talbot fall in battle,
I could well be persuaded you were Talbot.

The Black Knight
Do your prophetic voices tell you nothing?

Joan They speak aloud within my very heart
to tell me that misfortune stands before me.

The Black Knight
Joan of Arc! Up to the gates of Rheims
you have pressed forward on the wings of victory.
Now let the fame you've won be enough for you.
Dismiss the fortune that has served you as
your slave, before it frees itself in anger.

It has no love of loyalty, and serves
nobody to the end.

Joan What do you mean,
to halt me in mid-career, my work half-done?
I shall complete it, and fulfil my vow.

The Black Knight
All-powerful creature, nothing can withstand you;
you have won every battle: but do not
attempt to fight another. Hear my warning!

Joan I shall not let my sword sleep in my hand,
till England's pride lies vanquished in the dust.

The Black Knight
Look over there! There rise the towers of Rheims,
the goal you fought for and your journey's end.
The vast cathedral glitters in the light,
which you will enter in triumph, and where you
will crown your King, and so fulfil your vow.
Do not go in there! Turn back! Hear my warning!

Joan What creature are you, double-tongued and false,
trying to frighten me and to confuse me?
How do you dare commit the treachery
of bringing me false prophecies?

[*The* BLACK KNIGHT *makes to go, but* JOAN *steps across his path*]

No! stay
and answer me, or perish at my hands!

[*She is about to aim a blow at him*]

The Black Knight
[*Touches her with his hand: she stands motionless*]
Kill what can be killed!

[*Darkness, thunder and lightning. The* BLACK KNIGHT *sinks out of sight*]

Joan [*Stands amazed at first, but soon recovers herself*]
That was no living creature – an illusion
of Hell is what it was, or some rebellious
demon that came up from the pit of fire
to shake my steadfast heart from its foundations.
Armed with the sword of God, who should I fear?
I shall complete my task victorious.
And should they summon all the hosts of Hell
to fight for them, my courage shall not fail.

[*She starts to go. Enter* LIONEL]

Lionel
Turn, you damned witch, turn and prepare to fight.
Both of us shall not leave this place alive.
The best men of my people you have killed,
the noble Talbot breathed out his great soul
here in my arms, and I shall have revenge
for him, or if not, share his destiny.
And so that you may know who brings you fame
whether he wins or dies – my name is Lionel,
last of our army's princes, and unconquered.

[*He attacks her. After a short fight she knocks the sword out of his hand*]

Damn my ill-fortune!

[*He struggles with her*]

[JOAN *seizes him from behind by the crest of his helmet and pulls the helmet violently off, so that his face is exposed, at the same time brandishing her sword in her right hand*]

Joan
Die as you would have killed!
The Blessed Virgin kills you now, through me!

[*At this moment she looks him in the face; the sight affects her: she stands without moving, then slowly lets her arm fall*]

Lionel
Why do you hesitate? Why do you not strike?
You've killed my fame, now take my life as well.
I am in your hands, and I ask no quarter.

[*She gestures to him to escape*]

Escape? Owe my life to you? I prefer death!

Joan
[*Her face turned away*]
Save yourself! I do not want to think
your life was in my power.

Lionel
I hate both you,
and what you offer. I do not want mercy.
Now kill the enemy who detests you, and
who would have killed you.

Joan
Kill me, then – and run!

Lionel
Ha! What is this?

Joan
[*Hiding her face*]
Alas!

Lionel They say you kill
all Englishmen you take in battle. Why
are you sparing only me?

Joan [*Raises her sword to him suddenly, but lowers it again quickly, as she looks into his face*]
Oh, Holy Virgin!

Lionel Why call on her? She does not know you. Heaven
is ignorant of you.

Joan [*In the most violent anxiety*]
What have I done?
My vow is broken!

[*She wrings her hands in despair*]

Lionel [*Looks at her with sympathy, and goes up to her*]
Poor unhappy girl!
I'm sorry for you. And I'm touched. You showed
magnanimity to me alone.
I feel my hatred vanishing, and all
I know is that I feel compassion for you.
Who are you? Where do you come from?

Joan Go away!
Make your escape!

Lionel I feel compassion for
your beauty and your youth. The sight of you
strikes to my heart. I want so much to save you.
How can I do it? Tell me how? Come! Come!
Abandon this appalling covenant –
throw down your weapons.

Joan I am no longer worthy
to carry them.

Lionel Then throw them down now, quickly,
and follow me!

Joan [*With horror*]
Follow you?

Lionel Yes. You can be saved.
Follow me, and I will save you, but
no more delay. I feel unutterable
sorrow for you, a nameless longing for
your safety . . .

[*He lays hold on her arm*]

Joan Here comes the Bastard! Yes! They're looking for me.
If they should find you here . . .

Lionel I shall protect you!

Joan If you die at their hands, I should die too.

Lionel Then you do feel for me?

Joan Oh saints in Heaven!

Lionel Shall I see you again? Or hear from you?

Joan No! Never!

Lionel This sword shall be my guarantee
of seeing you again.

[*He snatches her sword from her*]

Joan How dare you! You are mad!

Lionel Now I must yield to force, but we shall meet again!

[*He goes out. Enter* DUNOIS *and* LA HIRE]

La Hire It is her! She's alive!

Dunois Joan: have no fear.
Your friends are here and powerful at your side.

La Hire Was that not Lionel?

Dunois Let him escape.
Joan, the cause of righteousness has triumphed.
The gates of Rheims are opened, and all the people
are cheering and running out to meet their king.

La Hire What is the matter? She's gone white: she's fainted!

[JOAN *staggers and is about to fall*]

Dunois She has been wounded – take her armour off –
it's on her arm: a superficial wound.

La Hire There's quite a lot of blood.

Joan Oh, if my life
could stream forth with it!

[*She lies unconscious in* LA HIRE*'s arms*]

Act 4

Scene 1

[*A festively decorated hall, the pillars festooned: off-stage the sound of flutes and oboes*]

Joan

The storm of war is hushed: on every side
singing and dancing follow the bloody fight.
Streets hum with riot: arms are laid aside:
green branches rear themselves, and stand upright
to make triumphal arches: columns are tied
with garlands, while the churches blaze with light.
The whole of Rheims cannot make room for all
the guests who flood in to the festival.

One joy, one thought, one feeling lights a flame
in every heart, and all those who of late
were enemies, now happily exclaim
in general joy, who once felt partial hate.
And every man who says he bears the name
of Frenchman, feels a pride in his estate.
New glory shines about the ancient crown,
as France pays homage to her royal son.

But I, who brought these glorious things about,
I have no part in this festivity.
My heart is changed, and turned quite inside out,
my eyes gone over to the enemy.
From all this happiness my heart takes flight,
and in the English camp finds sanctuary.
Out of the happy circle I must tread
to hide the guilt that laps my heart like lead.

Who? I? Is the image of a man
fixed in this pure heart of mine?
Filled with Heaven's grace, how can
it beat with love less than divine?
Warrior at God's right hand,
I brought salvation to my land:
now I love an enemy,
there, where the chaste sun may see,
why am I not destroyed by shame?

[*The music behind the scene changes to a soft, melting tune*]

Oh, the pain! The pain! That music!
Every note strikes on my ear,
calling up his voice, his face,
as if he stood before me here.
Just to be back in the battle,
weapons hissing all around me:
in the fury of the war,
courage could be found once more.

But these voices and this music,
setting snares about my heart!
All the strengths I have inside me
melt in impotence and turn
to melancholy tears that burn.

[*After a pause, she goes on with greater animation*]

Should I have killed him? Could I – once I had
looked into his eyes? Then kill him? I would sooner
have turned the murdering sword upon myself.

Must I be punished then, for being human?
Is pity sinful? Pity! Did you hear
the voice of pity and humanity
with all those others, victims of your sword?
The Welshman – why was Pity silent then? He was
only a boy, and begging for his life.
The heart is cunning, and can lie to Heaven:
it was not pity by which you were driven.

Why did I have to look into his eyes?
And see the noble outlines of his face?
It was with seeing that your crime began.
Poor wretch! God asks for blind obedience in His tools:
you must be blind to do His bidding well.
Once you had seen, His shield was taken away;
you were entangled in the snares of Hell.

[*The flutes begin again: she falls into a silent melancholy*]

My shepherd's crook! Would I had never
exchanged it for a sword, nor heard
in the sacred oak tree's branches,
rustling, the holy word.
Mary, Mother, Queen of Heaven,
would you never had come down;
take away what I could never
have deserved, your holy crown.

I have seen the heavens open,
and the bless-ed, face to face.
But on earth is all my hoping,
and in Heaven I've no place.
Why did you have to charge me with
this dreadful task I must fulfil?
Must I then deny a heart
that's framed to feel, and by God's will?

If you must display your might,
choose those who, in heavenly light,
and free from sin, dwell all about
your eternal mansion. Send them out
who are immortal, sinless, pure,
who neither pain nor grief endure:
but do not send the shepherd maid,
the weak of soul, the sore afraid.

What did I care for the wars?
Were prince's quarrels my concern?
Free from guilt I grazed my lambs
on the silent mountain heights.
But you tore me from that life
into that of royal hall,
gave me up to guilt and strife.
Oh! The choice – not mine at all!

[*Enter Agnès* SOREL *in great agitation. As she catches sight of* JOAN, *she hurries over to her, and falls about her neck. Suddenly she recollects herself, lets* JOAN *go, and kneels in front of her*]

Sorel No! Here in the dust in front of you . . .

Joan [*Trying to raise her up*]
Get up!
What is this? You forget yourself, and me.

Sorel Let me! It is excess of joy that throws
me down here at your feet. I must pour out
my overflowing heart to God: it is in you
I worship the invisible. You are
the angel who led my lord to Rheims, and put
the crown upon his head. What I had never
thought to see even in dreams, has come to pass.
The coronation ceremonial
is ready, the King waits in his robes of state,
the peers and the grandees are all convened

to bear the royal insignia, and the crowd
pours in a wave towards the great cathedral,
where dances sound, and all the bells ring out!
This happiness is more than I can bear!

[JOAN *raises her gently. Agnès* SOREL *is silent for a moment, as she peers closely into the* MAID*'s eyes*]

But you are still so serious and austere;
you are the cause of happiness in others,
but cannot share in it. Your heart is cold,
you do not feel our joys: your eyes have seen
the glory of the Lord, and your pure heart
is not stirred by our earthly happiness.

[JOAN *seizes her hand violently, but lets her go again quickly*]

Could you not be a woman, feel like one?
Take your armour off, the wars are done,
confess you are one of the gentler sex.
My loving heart draws back in fear from you,
while you are still the stern chaste goddess of war.

Joan What do you want of me?

Sorel Lay down your arms!
And take this armour off. Love fears to come
too near this heart that is encased in steel.
Oh, be a woman, and you will know love!

Joan Take off my armour now? Just now? I would
sooner fight battles naked and unarmed.
Not now! May sevenfold steel protect me
both from these celebrations – and myself.

Sorel Count Dunois loves you, and his generous heart,
only susceptible to fame and heroism,
now glows with a holy flame for you as well.
It is so fine to be loved by a hero;
but finer still to love one!

[JOAN *turns away disgusted*]

But you hate him!
No, it is merely that you cannot love him.
What reason could you ever have to hate him?
We only hate those who have robbed us of
the ones we love, and there is none you love.
Your heart is calm – if it could only feel . . .

Joan Have pity on me, and on my destiny.

Sorel But what is lacking now to make you happy?
You have done what you promised. France is free,
and you have brought the King, victorious,
to the coronation city. You have won
fame for yourself; a happy nation does
you reverence and homage; all tongues speak
in praise of you; you are the goddess of
this celebration, and the King himself,
despite his crown, shines not so bright as you.

Joan I wish the earth would open up and swallow me!

Sorel What is this? What has caused these strange emotions?
Who can hold his head high on this day,
if you look downcast? I am the one to blush –
I, who compared to you, feel I am worthless;
I, who could never measure up to your great deeds,
your loftiness. Shall I confess my weakness?
It is not the glory of the fatherland,
nor the renewed distinction of the throne,
nor yet the people's joy in victory
moves this weak heart of mine. There is only one,
who occupies it utterly; it has no room
for more than this one emotion:
He is the loved of all, it is for Him
the people shout, on Him they shower their blessings,
it is in His path that they scatter flowers:
my beloved is mine, and truly, I am His.

Joan Count yourself blessed! You are so fortunate
to love where all love! You may lay your heart
wide open, speak aloud of your delight,
display it in the face of all the world.
This national festival is the festival
of your love: all those people flooding in
in countless numbers into the town – they share
your feelings, their communion consecrates them,
it is for you they shout, make wreaths and dance,
you are at one with the universal joy,
you love what brings delight to everyone,
the sun; all you can see is your Love's splendour!

Sorel [*Falling on her neck*]
Oh, you have understood me utterly!
I am so glad. I was mistaken in you.

You do know what love is; you express my feelings
so powerfully, my heart is freed from fear
and shyness, and goes out to you in trust . . .

Joan [*Violently disengaging herself from her embrace*]
Leave me alone! Don't touch me! You will be
infected by the presence of the plague!
Go and be happy. Leave me to hide my guilt,
my wretchedness, my fear, in night and darkness . . .

Sorel You're frightening me: I do not understand you.
But I could never understand – your dark,
mysterious nature always remained hidden.
Could anyone understand what terrifies
your holy heart, your pure and tender soul?

Joan You are the holy one! You are the pure one here!
If you could see into my heart, you would
push me away in horror, as a traitress
and an enemy.

[*Enter* DUNOIS, LA HIRE *and* DU CHATEL *with* JOAN'*s flag*]

Dunois We were looking for you, Joan.
Everything's ready, the King sends us to say
he wants you to carry the holy flag before him.
You are to join the cortège of the Princes,
and take the last place, closest to himself.
He does not deny, and all the world shall know
that this day's honour is due to you alone.

Joan I am to walk in front of him? Carry the flag?

Dunois Who else is suitable? What other hand
is pure enough to bear the holy relic?
You waved it in the battle, carry it now,
to dignify the joy of this procession.

[LA HIRE *is about to hand her the flag, but she draws back with a shudder*]

Joan No! No! Take it away!

La Hire What is the matter?
Frightened of your own flag? Look at it now!

[*He unfurls the banner*]

It is the same one that you waved in triumph.
Here is the picture of the Queen of Heaven

floating above the earth, just as you said
the Holy Mother had instructed you.

Joan [*Looking at it in horror*]
It is! It's her! As she appeared to me.
See how she looks at me and frowns in anger
burning from under those dark eyelashes.

Sorel She is beside herself! Come to your senses.
It's nothing real that you're looking at:
it's just a picture, made by human hands.
She Herself walks amid the heavenly choir.

Joan Have you come here to punish your poor creature?
Destroy me, kill me, take the thunderbolts
and let them fall upon my guilty head.
I broke my vow: I desecrated it.
I have blasphemed against your holy name.

Dunois Alas! What is all this unhappy talk?

La Hire [*In astonishment, to* DU CHATEL]
Can you explain what all this is about?

Du Chatel I see what I see. I've been afraid of this
for some time now.

Dunois What did you say?

Du Chatel I dare
not tell you what I think. I wish to God
all this was over, and the King was crowned!

La Hire What? Has the terror that this flag inspired
turned itself back to work its power on you?
Leave the poor English to quake at this sign.
To France's enemies it may mean fear,
but to her loyal subjects it brings hope.

Joan Yes. You are right. To friends it is a sign
of grace, to enemies a cause of terror.

[*The coronation march is heard*]

Dunois Pick up the flag, then. Pick it up. They have
begun the march. We must not lose a moment.

[*They force her to take the flag. She takes it with extreme reluctance and leaves. The rest follow*]

Scene 2

[*The scene changes to a square in front of the cathedral. The back of the stage is filled with* SPECTATORS. *From among them step* BERTRAND, CLAUDE-MARIE *and* ETIENNE, *with* MARGOT *and* LOUISON *after them. The coronation march is is heard approaching in the distance*]

Bertrand Listen! The music! That's them now. They're coming!
What's the best thing to do? To get up on
the platforms, or to press on through the crowd,
to get a proper sight of the procession?

Etienne We'll never get through that. The streets are solid
with folk on horseback, or in carts. Why don't
we step aside just over by these houses,
and we'll be able to see it all quite well
as it goes past.

Claude-Marie It looks as if half France
was here! The flood's so overwhelming that
it even carried us away, and washed
us up here, all that distance from Lorraine!

Bertrand Who could sit quiet in his corner, when
such great events are taking place in France?
God knows, it cost us blood and sweat enough
to get the crown put on the proper head!
And our king, who is the true and lawful one,
the one we're crowning now, he should not have
a worse attendance than the one in Paris,
him as they crowned at Saint-Denis. The man
who stays away today and does not shout
"Long live the King!" is not a proper Frenchman.

[*They are joined by* MARGOT *and* LOUISON]

Louison We're going to see our sister, Margot! Joan!
My heart's beating so hard.

Margot In all her glory,
that's how we'll see her, and we'll say: "That's Joan!
That is our sister!"

Louison I just can't believe
till I see with my own eyes, that this great person
they call the Maid of Orleans, is our Joan,
our real sister, that we lost so suddenly.

[The march comes nearer and nearer]

Margot You still got doubts? You'll see with your own eyes.

Bertrand Look! Here they come!

[The procession is headed by flute and oboe players. They are followed by children, dressed in white, with branches in their hands, and behind them come two heralds. Then comes a procession of halberdiers, followed by magistrates in their robes. Next come two marshals with their staves, the Duke of BURGUNDY *carrying the sword of state,* DUNOIS *with the sceptre, other nobles carry the crown, the orb, the staff of justice, still others bear sacrificial offerings: after these come knights in the ceremonial dress of their orders, choristers with censers, then two bishops, carrying the sacred ampulla. The* ARCHBISHOP *carries the crucifix:* JOAN *follows him with the flag. She walks with her head bowed, with uncertain step. As they see her, her* SISTERS *show signs of astonishment and joy. Behind her comes the* KING, *under a canopy borne by four barons, courtiers come after them, and soldiers bring up the rear. When the procession has passed into the cathedral, the march music stops]*

Margot Well, did you see her?

Claude-Marie In all that golden armour.
Walking with the banner before the King!

Margot Yes, that was her. That was our sister, Joan!

Louison She didn't recognise us, though. She couldn't tell
how close her loving sisters were to her.
She just looked at the ground, and seemed so pale,
and she was trembling under that flag she carried –
I can't say I liked seeing her like that.

Margot Well then – I've seen our sister now, in all
her pride and glory. Who would ever have dreamt,
when she was herding sheep up on our mountains,
that we would ever see her look so splendid!

Louison The dream of Father's has come true, that we
should come to Rheims, and bow down to our sister.
That is the church that Father saw in his dream,
and everything else he saw has happened now.
But Father saw some sad things, bad things too . . .
it makes me scared to see her grown so great!

Bertrand What are we doing, standing round here idle?
Come to the church to see the ceremony.

Margot Yes, come. We'll maybe meet our sister there.

Louison We've seen her now: let's go back to the village.

Margot What? Before we've met and talked to her?

Louison She's not ours any more: her place is now
with kings and princes – who are we to force
ourselves on her now, out of vanity?
She was a stranger to us, even when
she lived with us.

Margot You mean she'd feel ashamed
of us, despise us?

Bertrand But the King himself
is not ashamed of us, he had a friendly
greeting for everyone,even the humblest.
However high she may have climbed, she still
is lower than the King!

[*Trumpets and kettledrums sound inside the cathedral*]

Come on inside!

[*They hurry upstage, where they lose themselves in the crowd. Enter* THIBAUT, *dressed in black, followed by* RAIMOND *who is trying to restrain him*]

Raimond Stop, Father Thibaut, stay out of the crowd!
You'll only see a lot of happy faces,
and your unhappiness will only spoil things.
Come on, let's leave the city now, at once.

Thibaut Did you see my poor unfortunate girl?
Did you get a proper look at her?

Raimond Oh, please,
come away now!

Thibaut You noticed how unsteady
she walked, how pale and anxious her face looked?
The wretched girl's aware of her position:
this is the golden opportunity
to save my child, and I intend to seize it.

[*He starts to go*]

Raimond Stop! What are you going to do?

Thibaut Surprise her,
cast her down from her vain happiness,

and lead her back, by force if need be, to
the God she has denied.

Raimond Think what you're doing!
Do not destroy the very thing you cherish.

Thibaut If her soul lives, then let her body perish!

[JOAN *comes bursting out of the cathedral, without her flag. The crowd presses up to her, adoring her and kissing her clothes: she is delayed in the background by the mob*]

There she is now! She bursts out of the church!
It's fear that drives her from the holy place!
It is God's judgment which proclaims itself
to her!

Raimond Goodbye! Don't ask me to stay longer!
I came here full of hope, and leave here full
of sorrow. Once again I've seen your daughter,
and feel as if I'd lost her once again.

[*He goes out.* THIBAUT *retires to the opposite side of the stage.* JOAN *disengages herself from the crowd, and comes forward*]

Joan I couldn't stay in there – spirits pursue me,
the organ sounds like thunderclaps to me,
the roof of the cathedral seems about
to fall in on me – I must have fresh air.
I left the banner in the sanctuary,
I'll never, never touch the thing again!
I felt as if I'd seen my two dear sisters,
Margot and Louison, go floating past me,
just like in a dream. Oh! it was only
an apparition, they are far away,
far, far away and quite unreachable –
just like my childhood and my innocence.

Margot [*Coming forward*]
It is! It's really Joan!

Louison [*Hurrying up to her*]
Oh, sister, sister!

Joan It was not madness then! It is you! Let
me embrace you both – Louison, and Margot!
Here in the strangeness of the lonely crowd,
let me hug my dear sisters to my heart!

Margot She does know us! You're still our sister, then!

Joan And your love brought you all this way to see me!
So far, so far! Are you still angry with me,
for leaving you like that, with no goodbyes?

Louison It was God's secret mission took you away.

Margot Now you are famous, and the whole world talks
about you, you're a household word, the news
even got as far as our quiet village
and roused us to come and see the celebrations.
We came to see you have your triumph, and
we're not alone.

Joan Father! Father is with you!
Where, where is he? What is he hiding for?

Margot No, Father's not with us.

Joan He's not? He doesn't
want to see his child? You haven't brought
a blessing from him?

Louison No, he doesn't know
we're here.

Joan He doesn't know? Why doesn't he?
You're looking all confused, and saying nothing,
and looking at the ground. Where is my father?

Margot Since you've been gone . . .

Louison [*Gestures to her*]
Margot!

Margot Father's become
morose . . .

Joan Morose!

Louison Don't worry, though: you know
how Father is, with all his premonitions!
He will recover, and take heart again,
once we have told him of your happiness.

Margot So – are you happy? Yes, you must be, now
you've got so great and honoured.

Joan Yes, I am –
happy to see you, and to hear your voices
I love so much, which take me back again

to Father's meadows. When I drove the flocks
out on the uplands, I was happy then,
I might have been in Paradise: is there
no way I can be so – become so once again!

[*She hides her face on* LOUISON*'s breast.* CLAUDE-MARIE, ETIENNE *and* BERTRAND *appear and remain standing timidly some distance away*]

Margot Etienne! Bertrand! Claude-Marie! Come here!
Our sister is not proud: she is more gentle
and speaks more kindly than she ever did
when she was living with us in the village.

[*The others come closer, and start to hold out their hands to her:* JOAN *stares at them fixedly, in a state of astonishment*]

Joan Where have I been? No, tell me! Was it all
a long, long dream, and now am I awake?
Have I left Domremy? It isn't true.
I fell asleep under the magic tree,
and now I've woken up, and you are all
around me, all the people I am used to!
I only dreamt about those kings and battles
and wars, they were just shadows passing by me,
one's dreams can be so clear under that tree.
How would you get to Rheims? Or how would I?
I never left Domremy, never, never!
Confess it now, and make my heart much happier.

Louison We are in Rheims. It wasn't just a dream.
You really did those things – collect yourself,
and look around you. Feel that shining armour.

[JOAN *puts her hand to her breast, comes to herself and shudders*]

Bertrand I was the one you had the helmet from.

Claude-Marie It is no wonder that you think you're dreaming:
the things you have achieved could hardly be
more wonderful if you had have dreamt them.

Joan [*Quickly*]
Come!
Let us run away, I will come back with you;
back to the village, back to Father's arms.

Louison Oh yes, come with us!

Joan All these people want
to raise me far above where I belong.
You knew me when I was a little child;
you love me, but you do not worship me.

Margot Could you give up all this magnificence?

Joan I'd throw it all away, I hate the pomp
that separates my heart from all of yours.
I want to be a shepherdess again.
And I will serve you like the lowest servant,
atone with the strongest penance that there is,
for having vainly raised myself above you.

[*Trumpets sound. Enter from the cathedral* CHARLES, *in full coronation regalia, Agnès* SOREL, *the* ARCHBISHOP, *the Duke of* BURGUNDY, DUNOIS, LA HIRE, DU CHATEL, *with knights, courtiers and people. As the* KING *comes forward, everyone shouts repeatedly:* "Long live the King! Long live King Charles the Seventh!" *Trumpets strike up. At a signal given by the* KING, *the* HERALDS *raise their staffs to command silence*]

Charles Frenchmen! and friends! We thank you for your loves!
The crown, that God has placed upon our head,
was conquered by the sword, and it is wet
with the noble blood of citizens of France.
But may the olive branch now grow in peace
about it. Thanks to all who fought for us!
And for all those who fought against us, let
there be an amnesty; since God has shown
us mercy, let our first word as King be – mercy!

All Long live the King! God save King Charles the Good!

Charles From God alone, the highest king of all,
we do derive the crown of France's kings.
but we receive it from His hand in form
both manifest and visible.

[*He turns to* JOAN]

Here stands the one whom Heaven sent to give
you back your true, hereditary king,
and break the chains of foreign tyranny.
Her name shall stand beside that of Saint Denis,
protector of our land, and to her glory
an altar shall be raised.

All Hail to the Maid!
Hail to the Saviour!

[*Trumpets*]

Charles [*To* JOAN] If you are sprung from mortal stock, as we are,
tell us what we can do to give you pleasure;
but if your native country is in Heaven,
if in that virgin body you enclose
the radiance of a nature that's divine,
then take the blindfold from our muddied senses,
and let yourself be seen in all the brilliance
that Heaven sees you in, so that we may
adore you in the dust.

[*A general silence; all eyes are turned on her*]

Joan [*With a sudden cry*]
Oh God! My father!

[THIBAUT *steps out of the crowd and stands directly opposite her*]

Several Voices Her father!

Thibaut Yes, her miserable father,
the father of this wretched girl, set on
by God's command to accuse her, my own child.

Burgundy What was that?

Du Chatel Terrible things will come to light now.

Thibaut [*To the King*]
You think you have been saved by the power of God?
You are betrayed, Prince! Frenchmen, you are blinded!
You have been saved, but by the powers of Hell!

[*All recoil in horror*]

Dunois Is the fellow mad?

Thibaut No, he is not, but you are,
and all these people here, and this wise bishop,
all who believe God would reveal himself
in the person of a slattern scullery-maid.
See if she dares, before her father's face,
assert the cheating, juggling lie with which
she has deceived her King and the whole nation.
Answer me, in the name of God the Father,
Son and Holy Ghost, do you belong
among the ranks of the pure and innocent?

[*A general silence. All eyes are fixed on her. She stands motionless*]

Sorel God! She says nothing.

Thibaut No more she dare, in face
of that dread name, feared in the pit of Hell
itself! What? Her a saint, and sent by God!
It was dreamed up in an unholy place,
under a magic tree, where evil spirits
have kept their Sabbath from time immemorial.
That's where she bartered her immortal soul
to the enemy of Mankind, if he would give her
the glory of some passing earthly fame.
Have her roll back her sleeve, look at the marks
Hell put on her to know her as his own!

Burgundy This is appalling! But one must believe
a father who denounces his own child!

Dunois No, we do not have to believe a madman
who brings shame on himself by such an charge.

Sorel [*To* JOAN] Just speak, and break this miserable silence!
We all believe in you – we trust in you
implicitly. One word, one single word,
spoken by you will be enough for us –
but speak! destroy this dreadful calumny.
Say you are innocent, and we will believe you.

[JOAN *stands without moving.* SOREL *retreats from her in horror*]

La Hire The girl is frightened. Horror and surprise
have stopped her tongue. Innocence itself
would be struck dumb by so obscene a charge.

[*He approaches her*]

Joan, pull yourself together. Innocence
has a language of its own, a look of power
which blasts the slanderer like a lightning flash:
Rise up in righteous anger, raise your eyes,
and shame and punish the unworthy doubts
that have been cast upon your holy virtue.

[JOAN *stands without moving.* LA HIRE *draws back, horrified. The general commotion increases*]

Dunois Why is the crowd afraid? The princes, even?
She is innocent! I pledge my honour as

a prince for her. There I throw down my gauntlet:
will anyone here now dare call her guilty?

[*There is a violent clap of thunder; all stand petrified*]

Thibaut In the name of God who thunders, answer me!
Say you are guiltless, and deny that Satan
is in your heart: prove that I am a liar.

[*A second, louder thunderclap; the crowd flees in all directions*]

Burgundy Heaven preserve us! These are fearful omens.

Du Chatel Come! Come, Your Majesty! Let's leave this place.

Archbishop [*To* JOAN] In the name of God I ask you: are you silent
out of a sense of innocence, or guilt?
If it is for you the thunder speaks
then take hold of the cross and give a sign.

[JOAN *stands without moving. Renewed, violent claps of thunder. King* CHARLES, SOREL, *the* ARCHBISHOP, BURGUNDY, LA HIRE *and* DU CHATEL *leave*]

Dunois You are my bride – I have believed in you
since we first met, and I believe you still.
I trust you more than all these indications,
more than the thunder even, rolling up there.
Your silence springs out of your righteous anger;
wrapped in the knowledge of your innocence, you
disdain to contradict such foul suspicions.
Disdain it then, but trust yourself to me,
who never had a doubt that you were innocent.
Say nothing, not a word: just give me your hand,
in sign and token that your trust is firm
in my strong arm and in your own good cause.

[*He holds out his hand to her: she turns away from him with a convulsive movement. He stands fixed to the spot with horror.* DU CHATEL *re-enters*]

Du Chatel Joan of Arc! The king gives his permission
for you to leave the city unmolested.
The gates are open for you. There is no
need to fear harm. The King's peace will protect you.
You are to follow me, Count Dunois. There is
no honour to be gained by staying here.
What an ending!

[*He leaves.* DUNOIS *recovers from his stupefaction, casts a last look at* JOAN *and goes out. She is quite alone for a while.* RAIMOND *appears, and remains standing at a distance for a while, looking at her in silent agony. Then he goes up to her and takes her by the hand*]

Raimond This is our opportunity. Take it! Come!
The streets are empty now. Give me your hand.
I will show you the way.

[*On seeing him, she shows her first sign of feeling, staring fixedly at him, and raising her eyes to Heaven. Then she seizes him violently by the hand and goes out*]

Act 5

Scene 1

[*A wild forest. Charcoal burners' huts in the distance. It is completely dark: violent thunder and lightning, and, intermittently, the sound of gunfire. A* CHARCOAL BURNER *and his* WIFE *enter*]

Charcoal burner This is a cruel and a murderous storm.
The heavens threaten to pour down on us
in streams of fire, the daytime is so dark,
that you can see the very stars at noon.
The storm is raging like all Hell let loose;
the ground shakes, and the ancient ash trees creak
and bend their ruined tops. This dreadful warfare
above our heads, that teaches gentleness
even to savage beasts, so that they tamely
cower in their lairs, can bring no peace to men.
Mixed with the howling of the wind and storm
you can still hear the roar and crack of gunfire.
Both armies are so close to one another,
that nothing but the forest separates them,
and any moment things could end in blood.

Charcoal burner's Wife
Heaven protect us! But the enemy
were beaten hollow and scattered, weren't they now?
How can they come to frighten us again?

Charcoal burner That's because they no longer fear the King,
ever since the Maid was found to be
a witch, in Rheims, the Evil One won't fight
for us no more, and everything has gone
astray.

Charcoal burner's Wife
Listen! There's someone there. Who is it?

[*Enter* RAIMOND *and* JOAN]

Raimond I can see huts. Come on, we can find shelter
here from this terrible storm. You cannot stand
this any longer; it is three days now
you have been wandering about, avoiding

the sight of human beings, and you have
had nothing to eat but wild roots you've dug up.

[*The storm subsides: it grows bright and clear*]

These are kind-hearted people, charcoal burners.
Let us go in.

Charcoal burner You look in need of rest.
Come in, and welcome to what our poor roof
can offer.

Charcoal burner's Wife
What would a young girl want with weapons?
Well, to be sure, now, these are troubled times
when even women have to put on armour!
They say the Queen herself, that Isabeau,
is seen in arms around the enemy camp,
and there's a girl, a shepherd's lass, they say,
has been in battle for our lord the King.

Charcoal burner What are you saying? Get back in the hut,
get the girl something to revive her.

[*The* CHARCOAL BURNER*'s* WIFE *goes into the hut*]

Raimond [*To* JOAN] You see,
not everybody in the world is cruel.
there are kind hearts, even in the wilderness.
Be cheerful then! The storm has spent itself,
the sun is going down, and all is peace.

Charcoal burner I suppose you will be wanting to join up
with the King's army, seeing you're under arms.
Be careful! the English camp is just near here;
and their patrols comb the forest all the time.

Raimond How can we avoid them?

Charcoal burner Just stay here
until our lad gets back from town, and he
can take you down a secret way where you
will have no need to fear. We know the woods.

Raimond [*To* JOAN] Take your helmet, and your armour off.
They only give you away – and won't protect you.

[JOAN *shakes her head*]

Charcoal burner The girl looks very sad – quiet! Who's coming?

[*The* CHARCOAL BURNER*'s* WIFE *comes out of the hut with a cup. Enter the* CHARCOAL BURNER*'s* SON]

Charcoal burner's Wife
It's just the boy, as we expected back.

[*To* JOAN] Drink up now, gentle miss. God's blessing with it!

Charcoal burner [*To his* SON]
Are you back then, son? What news?

[*The* CHARCOAL BURNER*'s* SON *has fixed his eyes on* JOAN, *who is just lifting the cup to her lips. He recognises her, goes up to her, and snatches the cup away from her mouth*]

Charcoal Burner's Son
Mother! Mother!
What are you doing? Who have you taken in?
That is the witch of Orleans!

Charcoal burner and his Wife
God have mercy!

[*They cross themselves and run away*]

Joan [*Calmly and quietly*]
You see, the curse pursues me. They all run
away from me: now take care of yourself
and leave me too.

Raimond Me leave you? Now? And who
will be with you?

Joan I shall not want for company.
You heard the thunder up above my head.
It is my fate that leads me. Do not worry;
I will reach my goal without my having to seek it.

Raimond Where will you go ? On one side are the English,
who have sworn to have a cruel and bloody vengeance:
on the other, our people, who have cast you out . . .

Joan Nothing will happen to me, except what must.

Raimond Who will find food for you? Who will protect you
from savage beasts and still more savage men?
Who will look after you if you get sick?

Joan I know all about herbs and roots. My sheep
taught me to tell the poisonous from the healthy.
I understand the sky at night and I

can read the weather in the clouds, and hear
the murmuring of springs deep underground.
People do not need much, and Nature is
so rich in everything.

Raimond [*Takes her hand*]
Won't you search your heart?
And make your peace with God – come back into
the bosom of the Church in penitence?

Joan You too, you think I'm guilty of that sin?

Raimond How could I not? Your silence was confession . . .

Joan You followed me into poverty and exile,
you were the only one who has been faithful,
who bound himself to me, when all the world
had cast me off: you too think I'm an outcast,
who has renounced her God –

[RAIMOND *says nothing*]

Oh, that is hard!

Raimond [*In astonishment*]
You mean you really aren't a witch?

Joan A witch!

Raimond And all those miracles, you really did perform them
by the power of God and all his saints?

Joan How else?

Raimond But when they brought that hideous charge against you,
you said nothing! – Now you speak, but then,
before the King, when it was so important
to speak out, you said nothing. Not a word.

Joan I submitted in silence to the destiny
that God, my master, has ordained for me.

Raimond But how could you say nothing to your father?

Joan Because it came from him, it came from God,
and correction will come as from a father's hand.

Raimond But even the heavens seemed to speak against you.

Joan If Heaven spoke, that was why I did not.

Raimond With a single word you could have cleared yourself,
instead you let the world believe this error.

Joan It was no error, it was destiny.

Raimond You suffered all this shame in innocence,
without one word of protest from your lips?
I'm just amazed at you, I'm really shaken,
and feel relief from the bottom of my heart!
I am so ready and happy to believe you.
It was so hard for me to think you guilty,
but I could not believe that any one
would bear so terrible a charge in silence.

Joan Could I deserve to be God's messenger
and not give blind obedience to His will?
Nor am I quite as wretched as you think.
I suffer want, but that is no disaster
for one of my rank: I'm exiled, an outcast,
but in the wilderness I have learned to know
myself. It was when the glare of honours shone
about me that my heart was in such conflict.
When I seemed most to be envied in the world,
that was the time when I was most unhappy.
Now I am cured, and this great storm in Nature,
that threatened an end to all things, is my friend.
It has cleansed the world, and me: peace is within me.
Come what will, I feel no further weakness.

Raimond Come with me, now, let's hurry to make known
your spotless innocence to all the world!

Joan He who sent this confusion will dissolve it.
The fruit of Destiny falls when it is ripe!
A day will come to vindicate me, when
all those who cast me out and slandered me
will be aware of what they did in madness,
and then the tears will flow for my sad fate.

Raimond Am I to wait in silence, then, till Chance . . .

Joan [*Gently taking his hand*]
All you can see of things is what you see:
your sight is still made dim by bonds of earth.
I have seen immortality face to face.
God marks the fall of every hair from every head.

Look, over there, the sun is going down.
As sure as it will rise again tomorrow,
the day of Truth will just as surely dawn.

[*In the distance, Queen* ISABEAU *appears with* SOLDIERS]

Isabeau [*Still off-stage*]
This is the way into the English camp!

Raimond The enemy! We're lost!

[SOLDIERS *enter, notice* JOAN *and reel back in terror*]

Isabeau Why have you halted?

Soldiers Heaven preserve us!

Isabeau Frightened of a ghost?
Call yourselves soldiers? Cowards is what you are!
What?

[*She pushes through the ranks, to the front, and starts back as she sees the* MAID]

What do I see? What have we here? Surrender!
You are my prisoner.

Joan Yes.

[RAIMOND *flees with signs of despair*]

Isabeau Clap her in irons!

[*The* SOLDIERS *advance timidly on* JOAN, *who holds out her arms to be chained*]

Is this the fearsome dreaded creature, then?
The one who scattered all our troops like sheep?
And now she cannot defend even herself!
Can she do miracles only for her believers,
and turns into a woman when she meets
a man? Why have you left your army? Where
is Count Dunois, your knight and your protector?

Joan I have been banished.

Isabeau What? You have been banished?
The Dauphin had you banished?

Joan Do not ask.
I am in your hands – do with me as you please.

Isabeau Banished, for having saved him from the pit!
For putting the crown upon his head at Rheims!
For making him king over the whole of France!
Banished! Now there I recognise my son!
Take her into the camp, and show the army
the fearful ghost they were so frightened of!
That thing a sorceress? All the magic is
madness and cowardice in your own hearts.
She is a fool, who sacrificed herself
for a king, and now receives a king's reward
for what she did – take her to Lionel –
I send him France's fortunes in a parcel,
I shall be there at once.

Joan To Lionel! Kill me
here on the spot, but do not send me there!

Isabeau [*To the* SOLDIERS]
You have your orders! Obey them! Off with her!

[*She leaves*]

Joan Englishmen, do not let me escape alive
out of your hands. You must have your revenge!
Take out your swords and plunge them in my heart,
then drag my lifeless body to the feet
of your commanding officer. Remember,
I was the one who killed your bravest men,
who had no pity for any one of you,
who shed whole rivers of English blood, who took
away from all those brave, heroic English boys,
the happy day when they could go back home!
Now take your bloody vengeance! Kill me now,
now that you have me; you may not always see me
as weak as this . . .

Officer You heard the Queen. Do as she says.

Joan Must I
be made more wretched even than before?
Holy and terrible one, hard is your hand.
Am I cast out for ever from your grace?
No angel comes, and miracles have an end:
Heaven's gates are shut; God turns away His face.

[*She follows the* SOLDIERS *out*]

Scene 2

[*The French camp.* DUNOIS *between the* ARCHBISHOP *and* DU CHATEL]

Archbishop Prince, you must overcome this black depression.
Come with us. Come back to the King! Do not
desert the common cause at such a moment,
when new emergencies need your strong arm.

Dunois Why are there new emergencies? Why is
the enemy back again? All had been done:
France was victorious and the war was over.
The one who saved us you sent into exile:
now save yourselves! I have no wish to see
the camp again, where she no longer is.

Du Chatel Prince, be better advised, and do not leave us
with such an answer.

Dunois Du Chatel, be silent!
I have no wish to hear from you, I hate you.
You were the first to doubt her.

Archbishop Which of us
did not doubt her, and who would not have wavered
on that unhappy day, when all the signs
spoke so against her! We were shocked and stunned:
the blow had struck too deeply to our hearts.
At such a terrible moment who could remain
objective? But our better judgment is
restored to us; we see her as she lived
among us, and we find no fault with her.
We are confused: we fear we may have done
a terrible wrong – the King repents, the Duke
blames himself, La Hire is desperate,
and every heart is plunged in deepest grief.

Dunois She lie to us? If truth should ever be
made visible, it would have to wear her features.
If there is innocence, fidelity,
and purity of heart on earth, then they
must dwell on her lips, and in her clear-set eyes!

Archbishop If Heaven would only intervene and send
some sign, some miracle that could explain
this mystery hidden to our mortal sight.
But in whatever way it is explained,

one way or other, we are guilty men:
either by using the Devil's arts to fight
our wars with, or by banishing a saint!
In either case, the wrath of God will be
called down upon our most unhappy country!

[*Enter a* NOBLEMAN]

Nobleman There is a shepherd, asking for Your Highness.
He wants to speak with you most urgently.
He comes, or so he says, from the Maid . . .

Dunois Quickly!
Bring him in! He comes from her!

[*The* NOBLEMAN *opens the doors to admit* RAIMOND. DUNOIS *hurries over to him*]

Where is she?
Where is the Maid?

Raimond Hail, noble Prince! I am
most blest to see this pious bishop with you,
this holy man, protector of the oppressed,
and father of the lost.

Dunois Where is the Maid!

Archbishop Tell us, my son.

Raimond My lord, she is not a witch!
By God and all His saints, I swear she's not!
The people are mistaken. You have banished
the innocent, cast out one sent by God!

Dunois Where is she? Tell us!

Raimond I was with her when
she took flight through the forest of the Ardennes,
where she revealed her inmost heart to me.
May I die under torture, may my soul
forfeit its share of everlasting bliss,
my Lord, if she is not free of all sin!

Dunois The sun in Heaven itself is not more pure!
Where is she? Tell us!

Raimond Oh, if God has turned
your hearts, then hurry, rescue her – she is
a prisoner of the English.

Dunois A prisoner!

Archbishop Oh, poor unhappy girl!

Raimond In the Ardennes
while we were seeking shelter, she was taken
by the Queen, who sent her over to the English.
Oh, save her, as she once saved all of you,
from a dreadful death!

Dunois To arms, then! Sound the alarum!
Summon the army to battle! Let all France
arm herself! Our honour is in pawn.
The crown, France's safeguard's stolen, gone.
Set all your bloods, your lives upon the cast!
She must be freed before this day is done!

[*Exeunt*]

Scene 3

[*A watchtower, with an opening above*]

Fastolf [*Entering in haste*]
The people can no longer be held back.
They scream at us to put the Maid to death.
Resistance would be pointless. Kill her now,
and throw her head down off the battlements.
Only her blood will pacify the troops.

Isabeau [*Entering*]
They are using scaling ladders to mount the attack!
Do what the people ask, or would you wait
until in their blind rage they overturn
the tower and kill us all along with it?

Lionel Let them attack! As fiercely as they like!
The walls are strong, and I shall find my grave
under its ruins, sooner than be forced
to do their bidding. Joan, now answer me!
Marry me, and I will shield you from the world.

Isabeau Are you a man?

Lionel Your own have cast you out.
You are now free from further obligations
to your unworthy fatherland. The cowards

who sought your hand have all abandoned you,
not daring to do battle for your honour.
But I shall stand by you against my people
and against yours. You once let me believe
my life was of some value to you. Then
I was your enemy, now your only friend!

Joan You are the hated enemy both of me
and of my people. Common ground cannot
exist between the two of us. Love you
I cannot, but if your heart feels for me,
then let it work a blessing for our nations.
Draw off your armies from our territories,
give back the keys of all the cites you
have taken, and make restitution of
all you have robbed, free all your prisoners,
send hostages to guarantee the treaty,
and I will offer peace in my King's name.

Isabeau You are dictating terms to us, in fetters?

Joan And do it soon, since do it you will have to.
France will not submit to English chains.
No, that will never happen, never! She
would sooner be a grave for all your armies.
Your best are dead: think of a safe withdrawal.
Your fame is lost, your power lies in ruins.

Isabeau The girl is mad. How can you stand her ravings?

[*A* CAPTAIN *hurries in*]

Captain General, you must put the men up in battle order;
the French are coming on with standards raised;
their weapons shine and glitter through the valley.

Joan [*As if inspired*]
The French are coming on! Now, you proud English,
into the field with you! It's time to fight!

Fastolf Madwoman, I should moderate your joy:
you will not live as long as this day's end.

Joan My people will have victory: I shall die.
Those brave men will not need me any more.

Lionel Weaklings! I scorn them! We have chased them off
a score of times in terror from the field,
before this heroine fought for them. I feel

nothing but contempt for their whole nation,
except for one, and her they sent to exile!
Fastolf, come! we shall give them such a day,
as they've not seen since Poitiers or Crecy!
You, Madame, will remain here in the tower,
and guard her, till the battle is decided.
I leave you fifty men for your protection.

Fastolf What! Are we going out to meet the enemy,
leaving this maniac behind our backs?

Joan Are you so frightened of a girl in chains?

Lionel Give me your word, Joan, you will not escape.

Joan The only thing I want is to escape.

Isabeau Put triple fetters on her. I'll engage
my life on it, she shall not get away.

[JOAN *is fettered, with heavy chains around her arms and legs*]

Lionel [*To* JOAN] You wanted it like this. You forced us to it.
It's still your choice. Renounce France, and embrace
the English flag. You will be free: these madmen
who now scream for your blood, will be your slaves.

Fastolf [*Urgently*] General, we must go now.

Joan Save your breath.
The French are coming on – defend yourselves!

[*Trumpets sound.* LIONEL *hurries out*]

Fastolf Madame, you understand what you must do!
If the day should go against us, and you see
our armies in retreat...

Isabeau [*Drawing a dagger*]
You need not fear.
She will not live to see us in defeat.

Fastolf [*To* JOAN] You know what to expect. Now pray, if you can,
success attend the arms of France!

[*He goes out*]

Joan I shall!
That no one can prevent me doing. Listen!
The war-march of my people! How it echoes
deep in my heart, foretelling victory!

Ruin to England! Victory to France!
Come on, my brave, brave men: the Maid is near you,
she cannot bear the flag ahead of you
as she did once – she is bound in heavy fetters.
But from her prison walls, her soul swings free,
borne on the wings of your brave songs of war.

Isabeau [*To a* SOLDIER]
Get up into the watch-tower that overlooks
the battlefield, and tell us what is happening.

[*The* SOLDIER *goes up*]

Joan Be brave, my people! This fight is your last!
Just one last victory and they are defeated.

Isabeau What can you see?

Soldier They are already fighting.
A wild knight in a tiger skin has darted
out of the ranks, leading his cavalry.

Joan Dunois! Come on, come on, brave soldier, fight!
Victory is on your side!

Soldier The Duke
of Burgundy is making for the bridge.

Isabeau I'd like to see a dozen lances run
his false heart through, the traitor that he is!

Soldier Lord Fastolf's putting up a strong resistance.
They have dismounted now; they're fighting hand
to hand, the Duke's men and our own.

Isabeau But can't
you see the Dauphin? Don't you recognise
the royal insignia?

Soldier Everything is covered
in dust. I cannot make out anything.

Joan If he had my eyes, or if I was up
where he is, not a detail would escape me.
I can count birds in flight, I can pick out
the falcon hovering miles up in the sky.

Soldier Down by the trench there is a terrible scrimmage.
That's where the greatest nobles seem to be.

Isabeau But is our flag still flying?

Soldier High in the air.

Joan If I could just see through the cracks in the walls,
I would control the battle with my eyes.

Soldier Oh, God! What do I see! The general
has been surrounded.

Isabeau [*Drawing the dagger on* JOAN]
Die, wretch!

Soldier [*Quickly*]
No, they freed him.
Now the brave Fastolf is attacking from
the rear – he breaks into their thickest ranks.

Isabeau [*Putting up the dagger again*]
Your angel spoke.

Soldier Look! Look! They're running away!

Isabeau Who are?

Soldier The French and the Burgundians.
The field is covered with the fugitives.

Joan My God! My God! Thou wilt not thus forsake me?

Soldier They're leading off a badly-wounded man.
A lot of men are running to his aid.
It is a prince.

Isabeau One of the French, or ours?

Soldier They're taking off his helmet. Count Dunois!

Joan [*Grasping her chains convulsively*]
And I am nothing but a girl in chains!

Soldier Wait! Look! Who's that in the blue cloak fringed with gold?

Joan [*With animation*]
The king!

Soldier His horse is shy – it rears – it plunges –
he makes his way to the front with difficulty.

[JOAN *accompanies his words with passionate reactions*]

Our men are moving up now at the gallop –
they've caught up with him – they've got him surrounded!

Joan Oh God, have you no angels left in Heaven!

Isabeau [*With mocking laughter*]
Now is your moment! Saviour, save them now!

Joan [*Falling on her knees, and praying in a voice of intense power*]
Hear me, O God, in my hour of most need!
To you in Heaven I send my soul in prayer.
You can make cobwebs strong as great ships' cables,
to your omnipotence it is a trifle
to make these iron fetters thin as cobwebs –
if you so will, these chains will fall away,
the prison walls divide – you gave your aid
to Samson, when he was in chains, and blinded,
bearing his proud enemies' bitter scorn –
trusting in you, he grasped the pillars of
his prison, strained and brought it down in ruin!

Soldier Hurrah! Hurrah!

Isabeau What is it now?

Soldier The King
is taken prisoner.

Joan God be with me now!

[*She has seized her chains powerfully in both hands, and snapped them. At the same instant she falls on the* SOLDIER *nearest to her, snatches his sword from him, and runs out. Everyone stares after her in complete astonishment*]

Isabeau [*After a long pause*]
What was that? Did I dream it? Where did she go?
How could she snap those chains? They weighed a ton.
I would not have believed it for the world,
had I not seen it happen before my eyes.

Soldier [*On the watch-tower*]
Has she got wings? Or did a whirlwind come
and carry her away?

Isabeau Is she down there now?

Soldier She's striding through the thickest of the fight.
She's faster than the eye can follow – now
she's here – she's there – she seems to be in twenty
places at once! She penetrates the ranks –
everything is giving way before her –

the French are standing firm: they are regrouping!
Oh, God, look there! Our men have all thrown down
their arms, the flags are being lowered –

Isabeau What?!
Is she cheating us of certain victory?

Soldier She's pressing on towards the King – she's reached him –
she's pulled him by main force out of the fighting –
Lord Fastolf's fallen – the general has been taken!

Isabeau Come down from there, I wish to hear no more.

Soldier Fly, Madam, fly! The fortress is surprised.
A body of men is making for the tower.

[*He climbs down*]

Isabeau [*Drawing a sword*]
Then fight, you cowards!

[LA HIRE *enters with* SOLDIERS. *At his appearance the Queen's* SOLDIERS *lay down their arms*]

La Hire [*Approaching her respectfully*]
Your Majesty, surrender
to our superior power – your knights have all
done so – and further opposition would be useless!
Accept my services; give order where
you wish to be accompanied.

Isabeau Anywhere
I do not have to set eyes on the Dauphin.

[*She gives up her sword, and follows him with the* SOLDIERS]

Scene 4

[*The scene changes to the battlefield.* SOLDIERS *with waving banners fill the background. In front of them are the* KING *and the Duke of* BURGUNDY, *with* JOAN *lying, mortally wounded, in their arms, showing no sign of life. They come slowly forward. Agnès* SOREL *bursts in*]

Sorel You are alive – and free – and mine again!

Charles Alive and free, yes, but at what a price!

[*Pointing to* JOAN]

Sorel Joan! Oh, my God, she's dying!

Burgundy She is dead.
See how an angel goes! Look how she lies,
in no pain, peaceful as a sleeping child.
The peace of Heaven plays about her face,
no breath is left in her, but there is still
some warmth of life remaining in her hand.

Charles She's gone – she will not wake ever again.
Her eyes will never see the sights of earth.
She floats above us, a transfigured spirit,
no longer conscious of our grief or penitence.

Sorel Her eyes are opening. She is alive!

Burgundy [*Astonished*] Has she come back to us out of the grave?
Has she defeated Death? She's rising, standing!

Joan [*Stands upright, and looks about her*]
Where am I?

Burgundy With your friends, Joan, your own people.

Charles In the arms of those who love you, and your King.

Joan [*After staring fixedly at him for some time*]
No, I am not a sorceress. Be sure
I am not.

Charles You are holy as an angel.
Our eyes were dimmed; the veil of night was on them.

Joan [*Looking about her with a happy smile*]
And am I really back with my own people?
and not an outcast any more, and not despised?
They do not curse me, they look at me kindly.
Yes, now I see it all again distinctly!
That is my king! And that is France's flag!
But I don't see my flag – where has it gone?
I must not come without my flag. It was
given in trust to me by my great master:
I have to lay it down before His throne:
I can do this, since I was true to it.

Charles [*His face turned away*]
Give her the flag!

[*It is handed to her. She stands quite upright and unsupported, with the flag in her hand. The sky is lit up with a rosy glow*]

Joan Look! Do you see the rainbow in the sky?
Heaven is opening its golden gates.
She stands in glory amid the angel choir,
her ever-living son held to her breast:
now she holds out her arms to me, and smiles.
What's happening to me? Clouds lift me up –
my heavy armour's changing – I am on wings –
I rise – up – up – earth falls away so fast –
the pain is short, the joy is everlasting!

[*The flag falls from her hand, and she sinks down upon it, dead. All stand for a long time, speechless with emotion. At a slight sign from the* KING *all the flags are lowered over her, so that she is completely covered by them*]